AWAKEN OH BRIDE
A Daily Journal of Awakening

Copyright © 2019 by Rochelle Butler

All rights reserved. No part of this book may be reproduced or copied in any form or by any means, electronic, mechanical, photocopying, recording or by any information storage or retrieval system without prior written permission of the Publisher. Inquiries should be addressed to the name and address below.

The opinions expressed in this book are those solely of the author and do not reflect the opinions of Million Words Publishing or its Editors.

Thank you.

Published By:
Million Words Publishing, LLC
Enjoyed By You!
WORDS THAT LAST FOREVER!®
www.millionwordspublishing.com

Library of Congress Catalog Card Number:

ISBN 978-1-891282-29-4

Awaken Oh Bride
Printed in the United States of America

TABLE OF JOURNALS

Acknowledgments 4-5
Preface 6-7
Introduction 8-10
1. Daily 11-13
2. Awaken Oh Sleeper 14-16
3. The Tortoise and the Hare 17-19
4. The Vineyard 20-21
5. The Virus 22-24
6. Coming Out to the Lord 25-27
7. A Place Called Beyond 28-29
8. Wisdom and the Fear of the Lord 30-32
9. Oh, How He Loves Me 33-34
10. Small Foxes Called Compromise 35-38
11. Having Loved This Present World 39-40
12. Fly Oh Butterfly Fly 41-42
13. Wise or Foolish? 43-45
14. One Thing 46-48
15. The Way Is Narrow 49-51
16. Study to Show Thyself Approved 52-55
17. Draw Me 56-58
18. Ascend or Defend 59-60
19. BLESSED or Blessed? 61-63
20. What Are You Sowing? 64-66
21. Time Shall Be No More 67-70
22. Chastened in the Love of God 71-72
23. Disruption 73-75

24.	Wimps vs. Warriors	76-80
25.	Suffering	81-85
26.	Desperation	86-88
27.	Doors	89-90
28.	The Price Is the Same	91-92
29.	Capturing the Heart of the King	93-95
30.	KISS	96-99
31.	What Type Of Lover Are You?	100-101
32.	Wait! Gingerbread Man	102-104
33.	Get Out of the Ness!	105-108
34.	Safe on Home Plate	109-110
35.	Let's Keep It Real! Hell Is Real	111-113
36.	Will God Be Enough?	114-115
37.	Lest We Forget	116-118
38.	Don't Be Wasteful	119-120
39.	Choices	121-123
40.	Is the Wait Worth the Weight?	124-125
41.	A Living Sacrifice of Worship	126-127
42.	We Don't Back Down, We Pray Up	128-129
43.	Awaken and Arise	130-133
44.	Change	134-135
	A Message From the Author	136

Acknowledgments

First and foremost, I give praise and thanksgiving to my Lord and Savior Jesus Christ for His showers of blessings and wisdom throughout the penning of this book of journals. I thank all who, in one way or another, contributed and supported me through the writing and completion of this book of journals. Though your name may not be mentioned, you know who you are.

I am so profoundly thankful for my beautiful daughter, Tiffany Butler. What a blessing to be your mom. Thanks so much for your love and support. Thanks for your constant encouragement for me to follow the Word of the Lord to pen the book. What a beautiful woman of God you have transformed into right before my very eyes. You are my friend and inspiration. I love you dearly.

I would also like to thank my brother, Denzel Butler; no words can express what you mean to me. You had supported me not only during the penning of this book, but when I started my wilderness journey with the Lord, walking by faith, you believed in me. Thank you for your friendship and a great sense of humor; it has been my medicine.

I am incredibly grateful to both of my grandmothers who are gone though not forgotten, Grandma Pearl Belcher and Orphia Butler. Where would I be if it wasn't for your prayers and rearing me to remember my Creator in the days of my youth? Thanks so much, I can't wait till we meet again.

Also, I love to express my deep and sincere gratitude to my parents for the love and caring sacrifices they made for me. I have seen them struggle and fight through many challenges, yet never letting go of the Master's hand. I thank them for not letting go because I also was holding on to their hands. Today I am here, holding on to the Master's hand. 'Till we meet again, I send my love and appreciation.

Last but not least, I express my sincere gratitude to my Aunt, Boopie Jean Butler, who became my second mom in helping to rear my siblings and me when my mom was sick. I love you greatly; your love is an expression of Christ that shines brightly. Thanks a Million!

Preface...

More than seven years ago, I was facing a dilemma that ultimately led me into a wilderness experience with God. It was in the wilderness, away from man, that I found Christ. I, like Moses, was led into the wilderness due to what I was seeing and witnessing in the church at that time. Surprisingly, what I observed were traditional church formalities, for example, doctrines, business, religiosity, control, titles, and money over the true commands of God. Consequently, I became a person that was on the outside looking into a church that had become to me unrecognizable. Nevertheless, it was during this period that I lay much of my heart in prayer before God and said, "Lord, all I ever want to be is a woman after thine own heart. Lord, I want to know you." After that prayer, I heard the spirit of the Lord say, "It is time to go into the wilderness where I will shepherd you. I want you to throw out everything you've ever been taught in the church. I'm going to debrief you. I will put back what's pure for much of what you've been taught which is the knowledge of man without the acknowledgment of God." Talking about a shock to my system and a new learning curve about coming to know and walk with my God afresh all over. God assured me of **Psalm 32:8: *"I will instruct thee and teach thee in the way which thou shalt go: I will***

guide thee with mine eye." So far my Father has been faithful. To sum it all up He said, *"Except the LORD build the house, they labour in vain that build it: except the LORD keep the city, the watchman waketh but in vain." (Psalms 127:1)* I had become a house that man had built. For that reason, it was in the wilderness, He started demolishing my manufactured housing, and a house not built with hands began to be built.

Rochelle Butler

INTRODUCTION

What a day and time we are living in, a day unrecognizable in comparison to days of my youth. This age reminds me of the Charles Dickens quote from "The Tale of Two Cities," "It was the best of times, the worst of times." However, I would like to bring it to present tense. It is the best of times, the worst of times. It is the age of foolishness, the age of wisdom. It is the season of light; it is the season of darkness. Wow! How prophetic! Truly, I am encouraged that we were born for such a time as this. The Dickens' tale is one of truth for the current times, primarily for the church, the people of God. For instance, if I stop and compare the church of the 70s and 80s, even the Baby Boomer generation, I don't find much resemblance. At that time, I remembered the church had such a fear and reverence of God, the church mothers were like your birth mother and when they saw the need to look out for your spiritual or physical well-being, they stepped in. The truth of children - obey your parents for this is right in the Lord - was real and practiced.

The whole point I am getting at is what has happened? Everything that I once knew and was taught in reference to sound doctrines along with morals have seemingly slipped away and the spirit of ease has set in along with the spirit of the world. I mean is God not the same yesterday, today, and forever? Has His standard of holiness and right living changed or been outdated? Has Christ

changed His stance on love the Lord thy God with thy whole heart, soul, and mind, and love thy neighbor as thyself? Are these things no longer required? What has happened? I have come to the conclusion that those were the best of times, the age of wisdom, but somehow now appears to be the age of foolishness.

About six months into my journey, the Lord led me to attend a church service with a lady I was working with at that time. Near the end of service, the man of God walked over to me and delivered a word from the Lord in reference to where I had been, what had happened, where I was going, what God was going to do through me, and this journal is a part of that word. At that time, I didn't quite understand the word about writing a book, but in the seventh year of my journey the Lord spoke and gave clear directions what I was to pen. This journal is meant to be as a toolbox. You may not need every tool in this journal, but I am certain we all at some point in our lives need a tune up spiritually speaking and need to tweak some things in our lives, or should I say the Lord does.

The penning of this journal, Awaken Oh Bride, was written by a burden and calling from the Lord to sound the trumpet and awaken His people to the days and times we are living in. The Lord clearly instructed me that this journal is by the leading and guiding of His spirit and not merely a formality from a writer's or publisher's standpoint. The Lord's agenda is to get a message out in hopes to awaken a people, not so much proper formality, or

writing rituals. Our preparation to meet the Lord will cost us something; it will cost us our very lives. Just as we plant seed in the ground for it to one day grow up, its growth is a process of seedtime and harvest, so it is with us. We do not wake up one day and say, "Lord, I am ready and prepared to go" having not done anything to prepare. I guess we could, but we may not be satisfied where we could possibly end up.

Oh my! What a journey it has been and continues to be. Paul said that I might know Him and come to know the wonders of the person. I pray that the words in this journal will penetrate your heart and awaken things in you that may have been lying dormant. May seeds of truth sprout and cause you to find Christ in a new light. Let's get this journey started. Be blessed!

Journal 1 – Daily

I believe it's of utmost importance to start this journal by putting much emphasis on walking daily with the Lord and seeking Him. This journal is intended to be a daily toolbox (the Lord's Word), used in our progress of going after God into a relationship which leads to spiritual maturity in Christ. The beauty of owning a toolbox is even though you may not need or use every tool, they're there if you need them. The Lord's Word is sharper than a two-edged sword, the more we use and yield to it, the more skillful we become.

Time with our heavenly Father should be the Genesis (the beginning) of our day. *Mark 1:35 reads, "And in the morning, rising up a great while before day, he went out, and departed into a solitary place, and there prayed."* Yes, Jesus knew the importance of spending quality time with His Father, so my question is, "Are we following His example?" For instance, I find in times of daily communion with my Father I become filled up with Him until His love overflows. It is the overflow of Him that conquers the daily challenges and gives me daily wisdom amid confusion and chaos. Also, I find that I am not strong enough or wise enough to go without Him, meeting Him daily at His gates. *Proverbs 8:34 reads, "Blessed is the man that heareth me, watching daily at my gates, waiting at the post of my doors."*

I believe it is important and crucial for believers to watch daily at the gates looking and waiting for God. When I orchestrated my life, making my decisions without listening at the doorpost for His instructions for my life, I had nothing but issues and failed attempts of trying to work things out myself. We should listen throughout each day to become aware of how God deals and speaks to us, for the Word says, *"But he that is joined unto the LORD is one spirit." (1 Corinthians 6:17)*

In order for Him to shepherd us (daily instructions, life, and strength), we must spend time with Him daily. *Isaiah 50:4 reads, "The LORD God hath given me the tongue of the learned, that I should know how to speak a word in season to him that is weary: he wakeneth morning by morning, he wakeneth mine ear to hear as the learned."*

As the scripture says He awakens my ear to hear, so we must awaken our ears to hear and discern His voice from the many voices that speak to us, such as the voice of our feelings, the voice in our minds, and the voice of others. The great and comforting thing to know is that He will speak to us, but will we recognize Him, and be obedient to His voice (the Holy Spirit). Trust me, sometimes that is and has been one of the greatest challenges in my walk.

Many years ago, in my journey, I struggled with hearing and discerning His voice. Sometimes I would rise early to pray, and other times I would not. I ended up praying a lot on the fly, and I

might add with no great results or victories. Amid my struggle, the Lord awakened my ear to hear and I heard Him say so plainly, "The devil wants you weak and powerless." The Holy Spirit convicted me of my laziness and uncontrolled flesh, and the spiritual warfare that was waging against me. Believe me, that day I realized the devil was after me, and had kept me totally in the dark and unaware of the unseen war. Let me tell you, that was an awakening moment for me, and the reality that while we are asleep the devil is yet working to destroy us. One of the devil's greatest weapons is ignorance. I've heard people say so often, "What you don't know doesn't hurt you." I have since found out that statement to be one of the biggest lies told. The devil thrives on ignorance, and ignorance, if left unchecked, will destroy us.

After many years of learning that lesson, I am rising early and walking closer throughout the day with my Lord, listening to Him and cultivating a life and atmosphere for Him to dwell in. I encourage you my friends, let today be a new day on a new journey of walking and listening at the doors to receive His Word. I promise you it will be the best start to a new day and life. You will never be the same. Let's get moving!

Journal 2 – Awaken Oh Sleeper

The times we're now living in jogs my memory back to days I, along with my siblings, would sit around the kitchen table with my Grandmother Butler and my mother listening to them talking about Jesus while sipping on their favorite coffee. I can almost hear the percolator brewing the coffee and smell its fresh aroma. This memory is almost as real as the truths they shared around the kitchen table that the world has gone to hell in a hand basket, and get ready, Jesus is coming soon. Time is short. Being only eleven or twelve at the time, I took nothing they said at face value. My conclusion of the whole conversation was I have plenty of time before Jesus comes, and from my point of view, things did not look as urgent as they preached.

Now that I've aged and come through several decades, my hindsight has become twenty-twenty, and I understand why my grandmother spoke so much and so often about the coming of the Lord and being prepared. For example, the Apostle Paul unveiled this understanding of time by saying, ***"And that, knowing the time, that now it is high time to awake out of sleep: for now is our salvation nearer than when we believed." (Romans 13:11)*** To awake is to arouse. We must arouse from our simple nine to five daily routines, and begin to hear what the spirit is saying to the church and to individuals. We must return to God in whole-

heartedness and give Him complete government of our lives and ask Him to come make us ready in this preparation process as a bride makes ready to meet the bridegroom.

For instance, a good example of what can happen when we become complacent and affected by the world we live in is Lot, Abraham's nephew. Lot had become immune to the evil in his land, Sodom, and the Lord sent two angels to destroy it because of the wickedness. The scripture says, *"And when the morning arose, then the angels hastened Lot, saying, Arise, take thy wife, and thy two daughters, which are here; lest thou be consumed in the city's iniquity. And while he lingered, the men laid hold upon his hand, and upon the hand of his wife, and upon the hand of his two daughters; the LORD being merciful unto him; and they brought him forth, and set him without the city." (Genesis 19:15-16)*

Isn't it amazing that the angels told Lot to arise and hasten, but the angels had to pull them out? I often wonder what Lot's heart was tied to in Sodom that when the call to arise came, it fell on deaf ears. I can't imagine what caught his attention in a place that was so evil that he saw no need to make haste to leave it. If we as the church can't look around and see the state and condition of things and desire not to hasten the coming of the Lord, something is wrong. The call is going out today for us to arise because just as Lot's salvation was near, so it is for us.

Awaken Oh Bride

So, as we move forward in awakening out of our sleep, we need to make choices and decisions that will prepare us to meet our bridegroom. The day of preparation is here and now. Will you arise and make haste? The alarm is sounding. Can you hear it?

Journal 3 – The Tortoise and the Hare

> *1 Corinthians 9:24-25 reads, "Know ye not that they which run in a race run all, but one receiveth the prize? So run, that ye may obtain. And every man that striveth for the mastery is temperate in all things. Now they do it to obtain a corruptible crown; but we an incorruptible."*
>
> *Hebrews 12:1 instructs us, "Wherefore seeing we also are compassed about with so great a cloud of witnesses, let us lay aside every weight, and the sin which doth so easily beset us, and let us run with patience the race that is set before us."*

How many of us know we need to be pacesetters in this race, and we need to be consistent and persistent? We must condition ourselves to countless situations of life, such as obstacles, setbacks, and setups; and being a quitter will not do.

This reminds me of when I was a little girl; I loved the story of The Tortoise and the Hare (a story about a race between a slow turtle, and a fast rabbit). As the teacher was reading the story aloud in class, we laughed at the poor tortoise because he was slow. No one, not even I, believed the tortoise had a chance of winning the race, and thought he was wasting his time. Nonetheless, he ended up winning the race due to his persistence and staying on course.

When I ran track in high school, the coach would always say, "Just concentrate on staying in your lane and do not look over your shoulder to see how close someone is behind you because it will

The Tortoise and the Hare

slow you down." But as time went on and the more I ran; I came to understand what my coach was saying. I don't know about you, but when we look around and take our eyes off the prize, which is Christ Jesus, and we compare ourselves to others in this game of life we may lose the race.

What I love most about the tortoise is although it seemed he would come in last, he wasn't affected by what was going on around him. He stayed in his lane, kept moving, and most of all he was not distracted by the pompous hare. The tortoise is such a beautiful example of being consistent and persistent.

For instance, I have experienced in my walk with God, things and people are not always as they appear to be. I've encountered a great deal of hype, and I've concluded that it's good not to get distracted by looking around at others. Remember, conditions are not always as they seem. Although the hare was a sprinter, the race is not always given to the swift. We have no time to be as the hare - to run ahead, take a nap, and not be about our Father's business, regardless of how good it may seem that we have it. I often hear the old folks say there is always room for improvement and I totally agree. Let us remember we can start running in the race and finish our course as the Apostle Paul states in ***2 Timothy 4:7:*** *"**I have fought a good fight, I have finished my course, I have kept the faith.**"*

Awaken Oh Bride

The lesson we can learn from the tortoise and the hare is that the tortoise won the race because he kept pressing toward the prize of the high calling, which is Jesus Christ, and the hare lost the race because he took his eyes off the prize, Jesus. We need to know the danger of self-sufficiency. The Word says no good things dwell in the flesh, and our complete dependency must be on God. Please hear me - this walk with the pursuit of God and coming to know Him has got to be on a DAILY basis. I cannot stress enough that we must plan on purpose to fit our schedules to allow time with Him. If that is the price, we've got to become good managers of our time and ask ourselves:

- Is Christ worth me getting up early to seek?
- Is Christ worth me watching less television or to say like my grandmother would say Hell-ah-vision?
- Is Christ worth my all because I want to know Him?

If so, allow no one to waste your time, as it is too short and most valuable. May we never be the same after a Christ encounter. Come on Church, let us run the race with endurance, as the tortoise did, looking unto Jesus the Author and Finisher of our Faith. Be blessed.

Journal 4 – The Vineyard

THE VINEYARD: God's chosen people called and set apart unto Him. Set apart from the world and its influences. Christ, our groom, set us on a fruitful hill according to Isaiah **(See Isaiah 5:1-2)**. God fenced us in, gathered out the stones, and planted us with the choicest vine, Himself. He is the vinedresser.

When the Father planted us in His vineyard, He planted us in Him. Everything of His nature and representation should cause us, the vineyard, to flourish and bring forth good fruit. In **Isaiah 5:4** it says the vine should have brought forth grapes (good fruit), but it brought forth wild grapes and the Beloved has a problem with the outcome and condition of the vineyard and says, "What more could I have done? I planted you in me, in a good place, a place of life whereby you can flourish." If that is you, the solution is only a decision and a prayer away, REPENT, and return so you again can reconnect to the true vine, Christ. The outcome of producing wild grapes can cause judgment. We know that God chastens those that He loves.

Our walk with the Beloved Father is a daily journey of highs and lows, successes and failures, victories and defeats, overcoming and being overcome. If we are not careful, our attitudes and the way we handle our issues of life can shape and form us. Unfortunately, the outcome moves us into a place other than where we should be. Instead of flourishing with good grapes, we are now flourishing with wild grapes, which are our corrupt nature, our fleshly life, the life of our will, doing what we want to do, doing what feels good. The old corrupt nature slowly destroys us over time and sometimes without notice until it is too late. To put it simply, sin (our corrupt nature) is our kryptonite and it causes us to become the enemy of God.

Christ tells us to stay virtually connected to the vine. *__John 15:2 says,__* *"Every branch in me that beareth not fruit he taketh away: and every branch that beareth fruit, he purgeth it, that it may bring forth more fruit."* Purge means the removal of whatever is impure or undesirable, to cleanse, and purify. Purging does not always feel good and we have to be willing to yield to God's purging. We must stay the course and allow the process to run its course. Today's journey is only one step in a million. Keep walking and flourishing while there is yet time.

Journal 5 – The Virus

Can you imagine that if the CDC (Center for Disease Control and Prevention) announced there was a virus that had broken out and you were in danger of it becoming an epidemic spreading to you, your community, and nation, what would you do? It would scare many of us and rightly so. Whether you or I realize it, something comparable to an epidemic has been spreading since the beginning of time. It all began when our first parents Adam and Eve lived in the Garden of Eden and ate the forbidden fruit. Eating of this fruit caused all creation to be born into the epidemic-**SIN**.

It has become clear that a population of believers (the church), does not seem to fear this horrible infectious disease that is running rampant among us; especially for those who are living a lifestyle of sin and having great pleasure in it. This virus is spreading rapidly throughout the body of Christ, in our families, lifestyles, and the nations of the earth. The sad part of it is that sin is no longer feared despite the reality of its deadly effects. Sin acts as a secret Assassin, and its aftereffects hit us when least expected, unaware, and off guard. *Ecclesiastes 8:11 reads, "Because sentence against an evil work is not executed speedily, therefore the heart of the sons of men is fully set in them to do evil,"* meaning when justice is delayed sin will rule. Consequently, the only permanent alternative to sin is death. When the fear of the Lord is absent from our lives and is not being preached, a spirit of ease sets

The Virus

in which leads into spiritual darkness and blindness. The Word says whom the Son has set free is free indeed and not to be entangled in the yoke of bondage.

For many the whole reality of sin and its effect is out the window. If we stop to think about it for one sin Adam and Eve found themselves banished out of the garden. For one sin Ananias and Sapphire died. WOW! I am certain if we had those sudden effects, we would not take sin so lightly. Sin cuts us off from God, breaks our fellowship with God, and affects how we have fellowship with one another. Sin causes darkness when the words say in *1 John 1:5: "This then is the message which we have heard of him, and declare unto you, that God is light, and in him is no darkness at all."* I believe one of the most profound things about sin is when fellowship is disconnected with the Father because of that sin we now have aligned fellowship with darkness and the enemy. Fellowship with darkness leads to deception and we no longer can hear or know the true voice of our Father. Because this darkness leads us astray, it becomes hard to discern the true voice of our Father and we are led astray by the enemy. Sin has grave consequences and we must wake up and come to that reality. *1 John 3:21 says, "But whoever practices the truth comes into light."* God's word is truth. *1 John 2:4 says, "He that saith, I know him, and keepeth not his commandments, is a liar, and the truth is not in him."* My God, sin is a destroyer. It has been said, "Be killing sin or it will be killing you." I couldn't say it any better

than that. Something is wrong when the church becomes comfortable with sin and no longer abhors it as Christ does. Sin led our Savior to the cross as He despised the shame. Church, it is time we become delivered from the virus today. We can no longer experiment with **willful sin** and **light repentance.** When a person has truly accepted Christ, a conversion takes place as it did for Paul on the Damascus road. There was an instantaneous change when Christ came in. Just like that, the virus disappeared, and he became healed, no more ever to be the same. When I say gone, I am saying he began to work out his own salvation with fear and trembling **(See Philippians 2:12)**. Working out your own salvation is allowing the work Christ began in us to come to full completion.

When Christ may live and manifest in our lives, the struggle against sin weakens because you or I am no longer living, meaning the flesh or our fleshly desire. Today the physician of all physicians is present with the antidote. Will you allow Him to be your antidote, no more to be the same? You are healed, you are free. He whom the Son has set free is free indeed.

Journal 6 – Coming Out to the Lord

The call of God is going forth for us to come out to the Lord, for those that have ears to hear, let him hear. Some would say, "Come out of what?" "What do you mean?" "I already go to a church. I'm on the praise team, teach Sunday school classes, and go to prayer meeting and Bible study." Trust me, I get it, I totally understand, I used to think the same way. All the things I have just mentioned are mere activities, but are not qualifying factors that I have come out totally to the Lord relationally because God is more concerned about the internal. **(See Matthew 7:22-23)**.

Coming out to God is a completely laid down life. Laying down involves the submitting of my will, my thoughts, my ways of doing things, my dreams, my hopes, and my desires. May Christ have complete dominion so that His kingdom come, His will be done in my life at all costs.

Unfortunately, the religious spirit has crept into the church and has taken precedence over the spirit of God. God is relational. He's all about having an intimate relationship so He can give Himself to us in a way that calls us to be away with Him, hidden in the secret place where we become His friend and lover.

(See Luke14:16-24) where we see the Master offering an invitation. From the text, we see the Master bade many to come to the great supper, but those who were invited all had excuses why they could not come to the supper. I understand the excuses that

Coming Out to the Lord

each presented seemed legit in the light of everyday life, being the fact, we all have obligations. I believe had they known what time it was spiritually, had they known the Father's heart, the external activities they deemed so great would have become of no significance. The hidden inner life of a deep personal relationship, one of communion with the Father would have made all the difference. Communion is about dining with the Father which is what the invitation of the marriage supper of the lamb is about.

When the Master beckoned them to come, He was calling them to come out of familiarity, the things they knew to do. He was drawing them to Himself. We can see from the scripture in Luke 14:24, that none of those men invited tasted of the Lord's Supper. Wow! We must be careful of our choices.

Christ has warned us that unless we eat of His flesh and drink of His blood, we have no life in us. We must become partakers of His life. My brothers and my sisters, it is time to come out to the Lord and get back to the beginning.

The Father is inviting us to drop everything and come to the table and learn what it is to eat and dine with Him in order to make Him the center of our lives. I understand coming out may not be easy. I walked through that journey some years ago. Upon coming out, the Lord told me I will get rid of everything you know, everything you thought, and everything you have been taught your

entire church life. He went on to say throw it all out because most of what has been taught was from the knowledge of man—what he thought, his vision for his church, and his teaching was mostly junk. However, it wasn't as the Apostle Paul said "we preach Christ and him crucified." As time went on, I understood I came out of the so-called church and got in Christ; there is a difference. While going through this debriefing process and journey, I was in a state of loss because Christ moved me completely from the church for a season. At first it was a challenge for me to become completely still and totally trusting in God. However, I found God for real and through this process my whole life changed.

Are you ready, my friend, to come out wholeheartedly to the Lord regardless of the price? To know Him is to love Him, to love Him is to obey Him, forsaking all others and anything that hinders or distracts. It will cost you everything, but is He not worth it? Supper is prepared.

Journal 7 – A Place Called Beyond

Have you heard the phrase, "It is beyond my control?" Oh, I have used that phrase hundreds of times when my back was pinned to the wall of my challenging circumstances, woes, and troubles. I even questioned God many times and asked Him, what have I done to deserve this? I looked at other people's lives, and from my view, it appeared they always had it together and everything always fell so perfectly in place for them.

However, mostly because I was trying to fix situations, I eventually realized I was in my strength, wisdom, and knowledge. Sometimes, I would get religious and confessing scriptures repeatedly like a robot trying to get things to change. I remembered a scripture that was once taught; **Job 22:38 that says, "When you decree a thing, it shall be established."** I mean I was decreeing, but my circumstances remained. However, after many days and weeks of seeking God on my journey, He began to teach me and give understanding to my confusion and frustration.

A central theme in the life of Christ has been we should no longer live for ourselves, but that we live for Jesus who died for us and rose again. My self-will of trying to fix things in my reasoning and understanding was not allowing Christ to have His way in my situations. God's way is not dependent on how we feel or think.

However, I began to see this dying to self moves us completely out of the reach of ourselves, our way of fixing things, our own way of understanding. Only God can be in control and not

A Place Called Beyond

us. ***2 Corinthians 3:5 says, "Not that we are sufficient of ourselves to think anything as of ourselves; but our sufficiency is of God."*** Apart from Christ, we can do nothing **(See John 44:5-8)**.

I love what ***Psalm 44:6 said, "For I will not trust in my bow, neither shall my sword save me."*** My God! Anything that we deem to be our bow or sword while trying to fix our problems won't do it to save us, only God Himself.

Christ brings us to a place beyond, beyond our own control, beyond our being able to fix it. This is a process of us dying that He might live. He takes us to a place beyond our ability to endure in our own selves that we learn to lean and trust in Him.

My friends, on this journey, everything is not meant nor cannot be decreed away because believe it or not God permits trouble to help mature us and to cause us to grow up. As we grow and become mature this allows His life to be manifested in us. I encourage you to let all frustrations go and any fixer-upper ideas you may have, it won't work. Rest assured God's got it all in control.

So, the next time you face a situation that looks hopeless, check in. He just may be leading you to the beautiful place called Beyond. Be encouraged. The sun will peek through the clouds of despair. I am certain you will find a rainbow in that place called Beyond. Bon voyage!

Journal 8 – Wisdom and the Fear of the Lord

One morning while in prayer I heard the Lord quote to me a scripture out of **Isaiah 33:6: "And wisdom and knowledge shall be the stability of thy times, and strength of salvation: the fear of the LORD is his treasure."** Upon studying I came to understand wisdom from the Greek interpretation is to be wise; skillfulness for living correctly. Biblical wisdom is God, who is the source of all understanding in all things of life.

We are living in times of uncertainty, so much upheaval, and evil in society and a people being forced to become silent and challenged on true biblical beliefs that are the bedrock of our society. It is hard to know what is true and what is false as so much deception has crept into our nation, church, and lives. It is like will the real you stand up. Having looked back after the Lord gave that scripture; I began to understand the importance and its relevancy for my life and the body of Christ as a whole. In these days of uncertainty that we now live in, we should make the Lord wisdom and righteousness unto us. It is imperative for us to make God our daily starting point in our quest for wisdom and direction. We must watch daily at His gates to get our understanding because we are not wise enough to choose ourselves. **Psalm 111:10 says, "The fear of the Lord is the beginning of wisdom; a good understanding have all they that do his commandments: his praise endureth forever."** To fear the Lord is to have reverence, terror, awe, and respect. To love the Lord is to keep His

Wisdom and the Fear of the Lord

commandments, which are an act of respect and reverence because we do not want to hurt Him by being sinful. We must love our Father. Therefore, sin is disrespectful because it goes against what He has taught us through His Word. Sin causes us to become a rebellious and stiff-necked child. I have noticed in these times of uncertainty people seem on edge and the least little thing pushes people to anger, rage, murder, and hate because as the Word says these would be days hard to live in.

Yet those that are of the body of Christ must become skillful in godly wisdom. We must walk skillfully and reverently toward God in our lifestyle, so we do not become drawn into places, situations, or battles that we are not to engage in. We must be the light in this dark world for those that may be on edge and out of control. Light will always overcome darkness. Our spirit is the lamp of the Lord where He will enlighten us and give daily wisdom for daily battles.

Ecclesiastes 9:11-12 states, "Wisdom is better than weapons of war: but one sinner destroyeth much good." What a scripture! WOW! Wisdom can do what war cannot do. How powerful is that? We never have to defend ourselves of those that challenge us or try to drag us into a knock down drag out over something that holds no eternal value. I love what ***Proverbs 15:1 says, "A soft answer turneth away wrath: but grievous words stir up anger."*** How mighty is that? The mere wisdom of a gentle answer deflects anger. I would say that is the skillful living I need.

Awaken Oh Bride

People of God, we are living in unprecedented times that will challenge and force us into decisions we never thought we would have to make. Making the wrong decisions in this time can cause grave repercussions that we may not recover from. The only way we can choose rightly is to first look unto the Father who is wisdom unto us and in us. Only He knows the end from the beginning. We can't rightly choose by only looking from the natural standpoint or with the thought and strategy of I did it this way last time, and it worked. We must look inside of ourselves to see outside, and see what it does not reveal to the natural eye. Let us look unto Jesus, the Author and Finisher of our faith, the One who was, and who is to come.

Proverbs 4:5-10: "Get wisdom, get understanding: Forget it not; neither decline from the words of my mouth. Forsake her not, and she shall preserve thee: Love her, and she shall keep thee. Wisdom is the principal thing; therefore get wisdom: And with all thy getting get understanding. Exalt her, and she shall promote thee: She shall bring thee to honor, when thou dost embrace her. She shall give to thine head an ornament of grace: A crown of glory shall she deliver to thee. Hear, O my son, and receive my sayings; And the years of thy life shall be many."

Journal 9 – Oh, How He Loves Me

When I think of the story of the cross, it reminds me of a love story. It seems from generation to generation that every woman loves the fairytale of Cinderella. Like most women, we all want to find our prince, fall in love, and live happily ever after. To think there is someone for us and meant only for us just as the shoe only fit Cinderella's foot. It happens every day.

Now let's move on to the ultimate love story of our Savior the Lord Jesus Christ. He gave up His life, hung, bled, and died that we might live. The most beautiful thing about His love story is that He died for all knowing that not all would receive His love and desire to become one in union with Him. I can't imagine what it would be for a groom to get to the altar on the wedding day and the bride decide at the last minute that I have changed my mind, and I am not sure I am in love with you. What a nightmare that would be.

Our heavenly Father decided from the beginning that He loves people enough that He will look beyond their faults just to meet their needs. He decided from the beginning that His love is unconditional and nothing that we could or would ever do would change that. Oh, how beautiful! He already decided that even if we don't receive His ring and say yes to His proposal, He would still give all for us. Today, He stands with His hand extended at the altar waiting for us to renew our vows and commitment and be willing to go a little deeper in our relationship of love with Him. If we say yes, He stands ready to whisk us off our feet into a total new day, a new beginning. No one can love us greater than God. No one can love us the way He loves us because His love is eternal.

Although human love can be fickle, it can sadly and quickly turn into an on again off again relationship. However, the most beautiful thing about this love story is it is not a fairytale. It is real, and it is something we can choose to have. ***John 3:16 tells us, "For God so loved the world, that he gave his only begotten Son, that whosoever believeth in him should not perish, but have everlasting life."*** Jesus loves me this I know for the Bible tells me so.

If that shoe of love fits your foot perfectly as the shoe fit Cinderella's, I dare you to put on the shoe today and allow Christ to whisk you off your feet into a life you never thought possible. Today is a good day to renew your vows. I promise you; He will not disappoint you. It's almost midnight. Your groom on His fiery chariot is waiting. Hang on for the ride and hold on to the ring.

Journal 10 – Small Foxes Called Compromise

Take a moment and reflect on your life. Have you ever gone through a tough situation and felt helpless? Helpless to the point to where you felt the weight of the situation was pushing you to a place beyond what is good, right, or spiritual. Many times, I have found myself helpless in a trial that tried to waste me completely. However, I knew that the only way it could waste me was if I willed to yield to the flesh instead of allowing the life of Christ to arise in me to destroy the enemy of self. I now understand and see the light as stated in **Luke 22:44: *"And being in an agony he prayed more earnestly: and his sweat was as it were great drops of blood falling down to the ground."*** Christ was in a battle as He was facing crucifixion. He was in a struggle with Himself. I am certain as we are living and breathing, we all have been in similar situations, certainly not to the extreme that Christ encountered.

Sometimes in my life when the pressure to do the right thing was so great I compromised my belief which caused me to fail and later regret my decision. However, I thank God for His unending mercy and forgiveness to remain faithful when I failed. ***Song of Solomon 2:15 says, "The little foxes spoil the vine."*** I like to think of compromise as a small fox. The fox compromised the vine in Song of Solomon by spoiling the roots of the vine, making them weak causing the tender grapes not to get the required nourishment at their most critical stage of growth. To compromise is to allow

Small Foxes Called Compromise

our principles or standards to be weakened and eventually it will put out the light of Christ in us. Compromise eats away our spiritual fruit each time we give into it. I am sure you have heard the phrase, "Sly as a fox." The fox gained this reputation of being sly because it's very calculating in its hunting skill by using deceit. In my daily walk on this journey, compromise is sly and if not careful can go unnoticed.

When I say sly meaning whenever I have given into compromise it seemed to at first not impact my life, but that allowed compromising in my life to become easier and easier. The effects of the compromise caused me to slowly become blind and ineffective in my relationship with Christ and halted the growth and increase of Christ in my life. Light and dark, sin and compromise can't cohabit with one another for a positive outcome because compromise is sin, though its effects do not seem blatantly noticeable at first. It is very sly. When I was a kid coming up, we used to sing the song with the following lyrics, *don't let the devil ride, if you let him ride, he will want to drive, don't let him ride.* I tell you! At the time I had no clue what I was singing, but boy did I come to understand the true meaning of the song as I began to grow in the Lord.

The devil is forever and always looking for a cracked door or entry point in our lives. That is all he needs, an opening in hopes to gain a greater foothold through compromise in our lives. Each time we compromise it becomes easier and easier to do if we do not

Awaken Oh Bride

take a firm stand in obedience to God's Word and resist it. One of the most striking things I realize about compromise is that it comes with a price. I am sure you have heard the phrase, "When we sin it's compared to signing our name to a blank check because we don't know what the price will be." I can't reiterate the reality and truth of that point enough, the reality is **sin is costly**. All sin will produce a penalty, though forgiven. Some sins or mistakes just have to run their course, unfortunately. As my grandfather would say, "A bought lesson is a taught lesson." For real!

Let us look at 2 Kings, Chapter 5. I would highly suggest reading the entire chapter because it will give you a good overview and deeper understanding to what I am saying. In 2 Kings, Gehazi was a servant to the prophet Elisha and was with him when he went to see Naaman. Naaman was a leper and healed of leprosy by the Word of the Lord through Elisha. Naaman, after being healed, offered the prophet gold and silver, **(See 2 Kings 5:16)** but he refused it. Gehazi for some unknown reason must have thought why is he turning down these gifts. I can just imagine the devil standing there waiting for the crack in Gehazi's life so he could get in and have a chance of tempting him to compromise. Unfortunately, that happened. Gehazi compromised. Gehazi said to himself his master was too easy and should have accepted the gifts and ran back to Naaman, lied and said his Master Elisha wanted the gifts for two other prophets **(See 2 Kings 5:20-27)**. I am uncertain if perhaps this was Gehazi's first time compromising his

Small Foxes Called Compromise

integrity, but what I know is the price he had to pay was one that **was very costly**. We see in **2 Kings 5:25-27,** Elisha asked Gehazi where he had been. Did he not know that his heart went with him when he returned to Naaman? Elisha said there is a time to receive money and a time not to. That obviously was not the time. The leprosy that Naaman once had immediately transferred to Gehazi and now he became a leper. My God!

May our prayer be today, Lord open our eyes to see you and give us a heart like yours that hates sin. Let today be a new day of no compromise, no retreat, no backing down, and in the face of compromise say, "My door is closed to compromise, devil you're defeated!" We have found the small foxes. Amen.

Journal 11 – Having Loved This Present World

Let us pause for the cause and think back to when Christ first captured our hearts and set them on fire for Him. Sometimes, we remember a song or place that connects us to a memory. I think back to a cold January day while in church many years ago, I was a prodigal and returned to my heavenly Father. On that January day, the reality of God's love for me became alive in my heart, profoundly and lovingly. Touched by His love, I started on a journey to fall deeper in love with Him. However, falling deeply in love with Him has come by journey of tests, trials, temptations, and great victories. That day I decided I was going all the way. Although I knew there would be many challenges along the way, I knew that God loved me and was with me. As time unveiled, I captured a new glimpse and facet of God's love, and in those moments, everything began to change.

Most importantly, change is the keyword! Many things in my life changed that I no longer did, especially things that did not please my heavenly Father. Such as some places I used to go, I no longer went, nor did I have a desire. I used to do things that others did even though I knew it was not right, but no more. My desires and spiritual taste buds changed, and so did my circle of acquaintances and friends. When I accepted the fact that not everyone was going all the way with God, meaning some were trying to serve God and the world with one foot in the church and one foot out. I like to call it double-dipping, the love and pleasure

of the world still had a hold on their hearts. From my observation over many years, most people love the world because it is all about the spirit of ease and no conflict, no spiritual warfare, and no conviction of the Holy Spirit. In fact, when you still love the world and tied to it, it is easy because you are not giving up your life. Therefore, there is no conflict. In Christ, there is a price. We are warriors on a battlefield, hated by the devil and his cohorts will do anything to see us destroyed. For instance, in ***2 Timothy 4:10 it says, "For Demas hath forsaken me, having loved this present world, and is departed unto Thessalonica; Crescens to Galatia, Titus unto Dalmatia."*** At one point in Demas' life, he was a servant of the Apostle Paul and ended up forsaking Paul. I wonder what happened along the way for Demas to love the present world more than God. I mean I am confident he at one point had experienced Christ and saw many wonders and knew Christ's way of life. Most importantly, being prayerful in this matter can keep us from making the same decision that Demas made.

May we be honest with ourselves and ask the following questions: Is the love of the world drawing me more than the Spirit of God? Do I enjoy things that God once pulled me out of, and desire to return to them because I love this present world? Am I comfortable in sin? Could it be sin has only separated me from the world externally, but internally the world is still in me? These are truthful questions to ask and may we allow the Holy Spirit to search and pierce our hearts for answers. Awake!

Journal 12 – Fly Oh Butterfly Fly

One day I was watching a special on the Monarch Butterfly and the one thing that captured my interest and I found so fascinating is their beginning. The most amazing thing about the life cycle of a butterfly is that it is first a caterpillar and goes through a metamorphosis before becoming a butterfly. The caterpillar spins itself into a cocoon where it is protected until it emerges as a beautiful butterfly. Wow! The amazing wonders of nature. ***2 Corinthians 5:17 reads, "Therefore if any man be in Christ, he is a new creature: old things are passed away; behold, all things are become new."*** Our union with Christ allows us to become new because it is no longer us that lives, but Christ that lives in us.

When you look at the butterfly, there is no resemblance of its past life. The metamorphosis of the butterfly should remind one of life in Christ as we go from the transformation of the old man to the new man. Our old mannerisms, ungodly habits, language, everything about the way we live changes because we leave the cocoon of the old life and fly off to a new life in Christ.

The life of Christ in all of our lives should be evident for others to see the distinctions from what we used to be and what we are now. Some questions to ask ourselves are how we treat people? Are we rude and unpleasant even though others may not always be nice or pleasant to us? Do we live a double life? Do we act one way at church and another way at home? Do we have the conviction of the Holy Spirit in our lives to convict us of sin? If not, something is wrong because the Word says the Holy Spirit was sent to convict the world of sin. We are on dangerous ground if we are comfortable with sin and call ourselves Christians. We must always remember **CHRIST IN US IS CHRIST THROUGH US.** If this is not the case then we must become real with ourselves, repent, and change, if not it will ultimately lead to self-deception, and self-deception leads to self-destruction.

It's time to fly oh butterfly and become a representation of Christ in this earthly realm. If you are still inching around like the caterpillar, it's time to get off the ground and start to fly. Be ye transformed by the renewing of your mind and prove what is that good, acceptable, and perfect will of God and fly on. Fly Oh Butterfly Fly!

Journal 13 – Wise or Foolish?

Back in the day, I used to sing in a church choir and there was one thing the director used to always stress that I have never forgotten, and that was "singing is about 95% preparation and 5% inspiration." Let us briefly look at the parable of the ten virgins which will give us insight into our journey of preparation.

> *Matthew 25: 1-13: "Then shall the kingdom of heaven be likened unto ten virgins, which took their lamps, and went forth to meet the bridegroom. And five of them were wise, and five were foolish. They that were foolish took their lamps and took no oil with them: But the wise took oil in their vessels with their lamps. While the bridegroom tarried, they all slumbered and slept. And at midnight there was a cry made, Behold, the bridegroom cometh; go ye out to meet him. Then all those virgins arose, and trimmed their lamps. And the foolish said unto the wise, Give us of your oil; for our lamps are gone out. But the wise answered, saying, Not so; lest there be not enough for us and you: but go ye rather to them that sell, and buy for yourselves. And while they went to buy, the bridegroom came; and they that were ready went in with him to the marriage: and the door was shut. Afterward came also the other virgins, saying, Lord, Lord, open to us. But he answered and said, Verily I say unto you, I know you not. Watch therefore, for ye know neither the day nor the hour wherein the Son of man cometh."*

Wise or Foolish?

To me the beauty of this parable is that God is so gracious, faithful, and patient. He is forever mindful. I am assured when we do our part Christ will always do His. We cannot afford in this day and hour to walk around foolishly. Being foolish can cost us as it did the five foolish virgins, who were not prepared to meet the groom. We must make the most of our time daily.

We are in a betrothal period, engaged to be married to our groom, Christ, and that takes preparation. So, today is a good day for us to stop and check our lamps to see if they need to be trimmed before we get to the door and find ourselves not ready like the five foolish virgins.

Our love and obedience to the Lord is what produces the oil in our lamps, a costly love, and a sustaining love that sustained those that had enough to meet the bridegroom at midnight. Firstly, I find this parable eye-opening to the fact all ten virgins started out with their lamps which indicated they had oil but the foolish did not fully prepare as the others to take enough oil with them. Secondly, another eye-opener is they could not get oil from the others that had enough because they said it will not be enough for you and me rather go to those that sell and buy. WOW! Church, this journey and walk with God is a personal one between you and Him because no one is going to be able to do your praying, studying, fasting, or anything else. Everything you and I need for our journey and preparation is not going to come from the pulpit on

Awaken Oh Bride

Sunday morning or on Wednesday night bible study. Remember it is 95% preparation and 5% inspiration.

In closing, I want us to realize that the church is not the Bride, but **the one that makes herself ready is considered to be the Bride** as the scripture says in ***Revelation 19:7:*** *"Let us be glad and rejoice, and give honour to him: for the marriage of the Lamb is come, and his wife hath made herself ready."* Understand there is a church within the church which is the Bride. Everybody is not going to be the Bride just as we saw in the five foolish virgins. The foolish virgins did not prepare or make themselves ready to marry the groom and that's a deep dose of reality. They all started out together as virgins but not all made it. I pray today you hear the sounding of the trumpet to awaken and trim your lamps while there is yet time. May your light shine bright in this dark world and be ablaze by the love of Christ. Be Blessed!

Journal 14 – One Thing

Have you ever been tested by our sovereign God or asked to do something by Him? Perhaps you didn't think it was that big of a deal because you didn't see the reasoning in why He was asking you to do it.

In the book of **Luke, Chapter 18, verses 18-22**, there was a ruler who asked the Lord what he should do to inherit eternal life. Jesus directed him to keep the commandments, in which he replied he had done so. Jesus then told him he lacked one thing (the one thing he lacked was eternal life), to sell all that he had and distribute it to the poor and he would have treasure in heaven. Then Jesus said to come follow Him. I am no doubt convinced that was a hard request being the ruler had many possessions. However, this **ONE** request was too great for the young ruler, and he turned and walked away. The Lord, though sovereign, did not violate the ruler's free will or influence him to change his mind.

On our journey we will encounter many challenges from the Lord such as this young ruler. Make no mistake, we will be tested and faced with situations that will confront the one thing in our lives we love the most, the one thing we love to do, and the one place we love to go, because God will test us to see if we really love Him. I have found that He will test us when we are not aware we are being tested.

Once upon a time, I was being tested but didn't know it. In my walk with God I have come to know and understand that He will

One Thing

test us in the things that lay close to our heart as He did Abraham **(See Genesis 22:2-14).** The test may not be as big as Abraham offering his only son as a burnt offering. Anybody that knows me knows that I am a big coffee lover and I love to hang out at coffee houses to read and talk to other people. I consider myself to be a social butterfly, a CC (Coffee & Conversation) girl. Well, one day the Lord told me to stop going to my favorite coffee shop; don't spend any more money there. I stopped going because I wanted to be obedient, and I love the Lord.

One day, after about a year, as I was leaving work and driving past my favorite coffee shop, I was talking to the Lord, and was saying I miss the good old days getting coffee there and hanging out. After a few minutes, I heard the voice of the Lord say, "Maybe I was just seeing what you would do." He got my attention. I was confounded and surprised. I said WOW because I didn't realize I was being tested. Well, the best part of the test that left me in shock and awe was when I got home and checked the mail. A wonderful sister friend of mine had sent me a coffee gift card to my favorite place and I just lost it (in praise). I lost it because she did not know about my test and her gift came on the exact day the Lord and I conversed, and He let me know I passed my test. I came to understand the Lord will test us in even the smallest thing that touches our heart. It comes down to who do we love, God, or our things. The Lord has so many ways to prove that He is Alpha (one) in our lives if we allow Him to be and He sure for sure knows how

Awaken Oh Bride

to show up and show out. To see God work and how He works blows my mind. That one thing that I love to do, God tested me. He tried my heart to see if I love Him more than what I loved and wanted—coffee and conversation.

MY PRAYER

Lord, I ask today that you come in our hearts and take up full residence. Reveal every area in our lives we still control. Help us to fully trust you and allow you to make us ready. Help us to know that our lives are safe in your hands. Come in Lord and build us your house, a house not made with hands. Purify our hearts and minds. Remove the blinders from our hearts, ears, and eyes. Restrain the present darkness that covers the light of you in our lives. Lord, we want to see you and be all yours. Send your fire to purge our hearts and motives. Help us to become one with you, the consuming fire. Teach us how to love you and allow your Son to live in and through us that your glory may be revealed. We lay our lives down at your feet; we just want you. In Jesus name, we pray. Amen.

Have a wonderful day and pass the test with flying colors. You can!

Journal 15 – The Way Is Narrow

Many years ago, I abandoned a fold at the behest of my heavenly Father which of course did not sit well with some because of their lack of understanding. Nonetheless, I moved forward with all odds against me it seemed. I have found along my journey to walk alone is a journey of great loneliness as you are treading new landscapes of life that you have never treaded before. I can in some way understand the children of Israel after leaving Egypt encountering hard and challenging places that caused them to doubt and have many thoughts of returning back to Egypt because at least they knew they would have food, water, and shelter.

Let us take a look at *Matthew 7:13-14: "Enter ye in at the strait gate: for wide is the gate, and broad is the way, that leadeth to destruction, and many there be which go in thereat: Because strait is the gate, and narrow is the way, which leadeth unto life, and few there be that find it."* This beautiful passage is full of so much revelation and life in it that underlies great instruction as well as repercussions if not adhered to. Usually when you find people in a crowd going in the same directions, they gain strength and confidence because they are not alone and do not stand out if something does not go quite the way they thought. It's very easy to hide in a crowd and be incognito, able to have your true identity concealed. The broad road is the way of the self-life; it's self-

The Way Is Narrow

serving to all its personal desires, homemade destinies, and everything else.

The way of the old life continues to lead you to do what you used to do, still live the way of your former life before you accepted Christ. The narrow way doesn't allow anyone to continue to govern their own lives, interests or desires because we no longer live but Christ lives in and through us. The narrow way will cost us something. It will cost us our very lives. Matthew tells us to enter through the narrow gate. Narrow is something that is small, limited, and contracted. On our journey with the Lord the road is so narrow that only you and the Lord can walk it, meaning you are able to walk it because you or I are hidden in Him. The road is not big enough for crowds or big enough for us to try and take our friends and family. Christ is our personal Lord and Savior that's why it's narrow. Abraham is a good example of this in **Genesis 12:1: "Now the LORD had said unto Abram, get thee out of thy country, and from thy kindred, and from thy father's house, unto a land that I will shew thee."** It's a lonely journey, my friends, that leads to beautiful destinations with the Father. This lonely journey challenges our love for the Master. It challenges who and what we love most and are willing to forsake all to follow Christ. That's simply the hard truth.

The Word says the narrow way is contracted by pressure and compressed. This narrow way leads to confrontation and disruption in our lives which causes growth and transformation as we allow

Christ, His life and nature to be formed in us. Think about it, the fruit of the spirit does not just grow and mature without going through a whole lot of dirt before the seed begins to bloom. As we walk this narrow way, we will journey and find new places in Christ we have never found before. We will find places deep within us that Christ needs to fill and rebuild as we journey through spiritual terrain of both warfare and blessings. We will begin to see the many facets of His divine nature and find out what He is really like without any interruptions.

My friends, I do not know what your situation is today or what road you are on. I do not know if you love the crowd or being a crowd pleaser. I do not know if you want to stay with your friends and go with them. Just realize, you don't have time to wait on no one, it's personal. I pray that you have found encouragement and strength today to make the right decision and change directions if you have found yourself on the broad road which leads to destruction. It's not too late to turn right and end up on a beautiful destination traveling alongside your Father. Trust me I have found no crowds are there. Have a great day.

Journal 16 – Study to Show Thyself Approved

When I was a little girl, my grandmother, Orphia Butler, was my Sunday school teacher. In her lesson plans every Sunday morning, she always included stories about what it is to be wise or foolish. We know to be foolish is to be a stupid person, one with an unbecoming character, and to be wise is to make good judgments in one's character. As she taught the class, she had a very watchful eye and didn't take any stuff. Any time one of us acted up, she would correct us that moment and say, "Who are you acting like? Who do you want to be, the wise or foolish?" She knew there was no better way of learning a lesson than one taught on the spot with significant distinctions between two characters and types of people.

As we studied in class, it became a part of our being and those lessons we learned back then, prayerfully, we carried over into our adult lives. In *2 Timothy 2:15, it reads, "Study to show yourself approved unto God, a workman that needs not to be ashamed, rightly dividing the word of truth."* The Lord requires us to be good stewards and doers of the Word of God. However, to be a good steward, we must first study the Word. The only way we can make the Word alive in us is to research and apply it as we come to know the author of the book and become encountered by His presence. The Lord said my words are spirit, and they are life. One day while meditating on this scripture, the Lord dropped a question in my spirit. He asked why Christians do not study my Word to be

Study to Show Thyself Approved

an active Christian while living down here. He said, "Look at how long lawyers and doctors have to go to school. Look at how much studying is necessary for them to be successful in their fields to become licensed practitioners. For them to be knowledgeable in their area of practice, they must study hard and also become disciplined. Why don't Christians take the studying of God's Word as seriously as people in secular fields?"

Sometimes, I have often wondered how much of the body of Christ has become deceived, and the spirit of deafness and blindness has taken over. When we don't study the Word, we can quickly become deceived. Just Sunday morning service and a weeknight Bible study cannot take the place of Christians studying to show themselves approved. When we study by the Spirit of God, we learn to divide the Word of God. In some sense, it is protections from deception. ***1 Corinthians 14:29 tells us "Let the prophets speak two or three and let the other judge."*** Imagine that, I wonder how often that happens? Sadly, I learned the hard way, but I learned. Think about it. I don't easily swallow pills or medication just because the doctor prescribed it, especially if I'm not sure what it's for and what side effects there may be. However, some of us so easily swallow every word of a preacher, teacher, prophet, evangelist, apostle, or brother so and so without studying to know what the Word is saying and finding the hidden truths in it before we swallow it entirely. The Word tells us to be careful how

we hear. I would guarantee if you study to show thyself approved, the spirit of deception that is running so rampant would not be.

Unfortunately, much of the church is lazy and expects the preacher or its leaders to do everything for them, but the Lord never designed it that way. Being a sluggard will cost us. **Proverbs 6:6-8: "Go to the ant, thou sluggard; consider her ways and be wise; Which having no guide, overseer, or ruler, Provideth her meat in the summer, and gathereth her food in the harvest."** We can learn much from this verse; the ant is not waiting on a Sunday morning service to gather her food for the week. She is busy preparing for herself day in and day out because she knows winter is coming. She's not waiting for a prophetic word from some prophet, teacher, or evangelist. She is preparing her bread (studying the Word of God), and eating the bread of life. The ant, though in a colony with millions of other ants, is still handling her business and not being persuaded or affected by what is going on around her. What about us? Are we not in a state of preparation to meet our bridegroom because we realize we will one day, if our Lord approves us? This is serious stuff.

Accordingly, we are in a day of awakening out of our slumber. I know this journey of life can be burdensome, but let us continue going after God. We must streamline our lives of anything that stops us from getting closer to God; it needs to go. The night is coming when no man can work. May we consider the ways of the ant and be wise? Come on now, let's keep it moving. Grab your

Bible, your pen, and your notebook to study and expect the Holy Spirit (the Spirit of Truth) to come, and teach you all things of life and godliness.

Journal 17 – Draw Me

I remember the days being a young girl and visiting my momma and grandmother in Mexico, Missouri every second and fourth weekend. My grandmother Belcher worked nights at a nursing home. Not long after she got off work, changed her clothes, had a cup of coffee, and off she went to close her doors and pray. She was such a godly, praying woman. I admired her for her life and relationship with God. Over the years, though she is gone to be with the Lord, her life has so impacted me as a young girl that I desired to be a godly, praying woman like her.

Song of Solomon is one of my favorite books of the Bible because it speaks of God's love for His bride as well as her love for the bridegroom, Christ. One verse that caught my attention was **Song of Solomon 1:4, which says, "Draw me, we will run after thee."** I say draw me Lord and I'll come running after thee. In my journey, this has become a constant prayer for my life, because I realize I do not have enough strength in me to be drawn away from myself, my thoughts, my plans, my problems, all of it. In addition, the Word says no man comes lest the Spirit draw him. The beauty of being drawn is if we draw near to God, He will draw near to us. **(See James 4:8)**

So, many years ago, I began to pray, *Lord make me a woman after thine own heart* and to this day I still pray it, and He has answered. When I asked the Lord to draw me, I came to know that I was giving Him consent to draw me and to come close, as He is a

Draw Me

gentleman, who waits and wants to be invited. He will not be intrusive and invade our space because we have free will. One day I ran upon another scripture that has shaped my life and relationship, **Psalms 63:8: "My soul followeth hard after thee."** To follow hard means to follow close and the only way I can follow close is to ask the Lord to draw me.

One thing that I know and am certain of and that is nothing just falls off on us. Nothing just happens. We have to go after it and become a God Chaser if we desire to go to new depths of love and have a relationship with Him. Right now, at this very moment, all of us can choose to be as close to God as we want. It is simply a sacrifice of love. We decide if we want a mere outer court relationship or an inner court relationship. Inner court is more intimate where we become the friend of God and He takes us into His secret chambers and reveals Himself and His secrets. Christ Himself is a mystery. In the inner court, He unveils Himself, as there are so many beautiful facets of our beautiful Savior. The Lord once said to me only two lovers can understand the love language between them. Everyone from the outside looking in may think it strange, but it's not for others to understand the love between you and your lover.

Just think about all the names that encompass our Lord, and how each name gives a different expression as to who He is. Such as ***Elohim (Mighty God), El Elyon (Most High God), El Shaddai (Mighty One), Jehovah-Nissi (The Lord my Banner), Jehovah-***

Shammah (The Lord is there). These are just a few. It takes time to get to know God in all of His many facets, but we must give consent and make room in the inner sanctuary of our heart where He resides. The Word says He makes all things known to His friends. We are in an hour where so many things are fighting for our time and attention and drawing us away from the things that matter most. We are in a day and time where we will need to be able to hear clearly what the spirit is saying and revealing. If we are miles apart in the spirit in our relationship, we will suffer loss. We must become more deeply and intimately acquainted with Christ.

Christ is offering you and me a personal invitation today to go a little deeper in our union and relationship with Him. Will we give Him consent to draw us? He's waiting.

MY PRAYER

Heavenly Father, we ask today that you set a fiery love deep within us for you. May we become one with you, the consuming fire. Please rekindle the embers of our love for you and by your love may we never be the same. Draw us and we'll coming running hard after you. Thanks Father, in your son Jesus' name. Amen.

Journal 18 – Ascend or Defend

In **1 Corinthians Chapter 13**, better known as the love chapter, which I absolutely love because it portrays the love of the Father so well. In verse 5 it says love does not take account of a suffered wrong, WOW! I found when I didn't take account of a suffered wrong; I was always ascending and not defending. Christ never defended Himself through all of His conflict and opposition. He just yielded to the life of His Father and allowed it to be portrayed through Him. That is the victory and we can do no less.

One time I had a situation that almost had the best of me. When I say the best of me, I mean where I wanted to take matters in my own hands and react from the old nature instead of allowing the life of Christ to prevail. As I was in prayer, I gently heard the Lord say, "Love doesn't defend, but it ascends." Love ascends above the hurt, above the pain, above the frustration, above the anger. Love ascends. When love ascends above everything of the flesh, the pain is beneath you and loses its power.

I understand none of us like to be hurt especially when we have done nothing to deserve it. Regardless, we can choose to ascend and not defend. I tried it and it works. I am reminded of ***Psalm 24:3-4: "Who shall ascend into the hill of the LORD? or who shall stand in his holy place? He that hath clean hands, and a pure heart; who hath not lifted up his soul unto vanity, nor sworn deceitfully."***

When we have clean hands and a pure heart, we ascend. When we love, we ascend. Regardless of what others do, we can't lose when we choose to ascend and not defend, I love it! Ascend my friend and rise on the wings of God's love. Don't be down on yourself if you miss it, it's a journey, you can do it, I believe in you. Give Christ room to grow in you. I encourage you from this day forth. Ascend my friend because you don't have to defend.

Journal 19 – BLESSED or Blessed?

Who loves being blessed? We all can say yes to that and be in agreement. I hear a lot of different clichés on the word blessed. For instance: I'm too blessed to be stressed; how are you doing today? "I'm blessed." The last one is I'm blessed because I'm living my best life. So, let's take a look at the word blessed according to the Word of God. As far as I can remember most if not all of my conversations with people in regard to blessed have equated being blessed to having a lot of money, living in a big house, having a huge ministry, so forth and so on. I am by no means saying those things are not blessings or considering one not to be blessed.

Let us peek at **Psalms 1:1-3:** *"Blessed is the man that walketh not in the counsel of the ungodly, nor standeth in the way of sinners, nor sitteth in the seat of the scornful. But his delight is in the law of the LORD; and in his law doth he meditate day and night. And he shall be like a tree planted by the rivers of water, that bringeth forth his fruit in his season; his leaf also shall not wither; and whatsoever he doeth shall prosper."* How beautiful! This narrative of blessed really is life transforming and has nothing to do with external wealth and riches. When we do what is listed above it says we prosper. According to the above narrative, the things that cannot be bought or sold are blessings and should be more valuable and necessary for life and godliness. Even at the end of the day if you or I give up our car, home, job, or money for Christ's sake, that's being blessed and a blessing.

Let's look at what being blessed is all about. **(See Matthew 5:1-11)** where we see the beatitudes of Christ, OMG! You are blessed if you are poor in spirit, mourn, meek, merciful, pure in heart, a peacemaker. *Matthew 5:10-11 states, "Blessed are they which are persecuted for righteousness' sake: for theirs is the kingdom of heaven. Blessed are ye, when men shall revile you, and persecute you, and shall say all manner of evil against you falsely, for my sake."* Rejoice! The word blessed also means to be happy. We can be happy when we know that we are Christ's children and He is our life and provider. The blessed man's delight is in the law of the Lord, and in His law does He meditate day and night and He shall be planted like a tree. Now that is being blessed my friends.

Earlier in my walk and journey as a Christian, I used to become so upset and offended when people would talk about me and say things that were not true, but one day I realized that was a part of the **BLESSED LIFE.** *1 Peter 4:14-16: "If ye be reproached for the name of Christ, happy are ye; for the spirit of glory and of God resteth upon you: on their part he is evil spoken of, but on your part he is glorified. But let none of you suffer as a murderer, or as a thief, or as an evildoer, or as a busybody in other men's matters. Yet if any man suffer as a Christian, let him not be ashamed; but let him glorify God on this behalf."*

It is time we come back to the center and get away from all the hype and clichés in the body of Christ. We are called to be sons and daughters of the most high God.

Awaken Oh Bride

- ♱ Blessed are we counted worthy to suffer for the name of Christ.
- ♱ Blessed are we to represent Him in this earthly realm.
- ♱ Blessed are we when we bless others by allowing the representation of the life of Christ to be lived through us.
- ♱ Blessed are we when the rivers of living water flow through us to others.
- ♱ Blessed are we to be the light of the world that shines bright in places of darkness.

WE ARE BLESSED TO BE A BLESSING!

Journal 20 – What Are You Sowing?

I once watched a documentary about farmers growing grapes in their vineyard. They spoke of some of the challenges they faced as harvesters. Sometimes they faced lower than average temperatures which created enormous problems which could kill their harvest. Some of the farmers said they stayed up all night to observe and protect their harvest using heating elements to increase the temperatures with hopes to save as much of their harvest as possible.

I understand this process of harvesting a good crop; however let's look at it from a spiritual standpoint. When we look at **Galatians 6:7-8:** *"**Be not deceived; God is not mocked: for whatsoever a man soweth, that shall he also reap. For he that soweth to his flesh shall of the flesh reap corruption; but he that soweth to the Spirit shall of the Spirit reap life everlasting.**"* The Word of God has a lot to say about sowing and reaping as well as seedtime and harvest. When we plant something, we expect to reap something, be it good or bad. When I was a kid, I used to love getting the box of candy that had a prize in it. I did not know if it was going to be something I would like or not, but was hoping and expecting something good all the time.

In **Galatians 5:19-21,** we see the list about sowing to the flesh. Let's look at the drama list of what the works of the flesh are: *"**Now the works of the flesh are manifest, which are these; Adultery, fornication, uncleanness, lasciviousness, Idolatry,**

What Are You Sowing?

witchcraft, hatred, variance, emulations, wrath, strife, seditions, heresies, Envyings, murders, drunkenness, revellings, and such like: of the which I tell you before, as I have also told you in time past, that they which do such things shall not inherit the kingdom of God." This list right here is a deadly list that we should hate because if we practice these things, we already know exactly what we will get unlike the surprise in the candy box. We know this because the Word says they that do such things shall not inherit the kingdom of God.

Now let's look at the list with the fruit of the Spirit in *Galatians 5:22-23: "But the fruit of the Spirit is love, joy, peace, longsuffering, gentleness, goodness, faith, meekness, temperance: against such there is no law."* As I was studying this scripture one day the amazing thing I noticed was the list was so much smaller than the list of sowing to the flesh. I understand because when you are obedient and you are sowing to the spirit you have far fewer self-inflicted problems. The beautiful thing is that all nine fruits of the spirit are powerful enough to combat all the works of the flesh.

As we go from day to day in our journey, let us be mindful that we are continually sowing to the flesh, or the spirit. If I plant peas of peace in my garden, I am not going to get smelly onions of attitude. Hopefully, I am going to get exactly what I planted. Let us be mindful of the words we speak, the actions we take, and the way we handle our business because we're always sowing. For

Awaken Oh Bride

as the Word says we all will give an account of every idle word spoken. I know it is a tough challenge, but when you choose to live life in the spirit under the divine government of God, you land in green pastures. Remember, the grass is not always greener on the other side, especially if you're sowing to the flesh. Sin is only for a season, but eternal life is forever. So, watch closely over the vineyard, and don't let the cold creep in and freeze your grapes. Enjoy your day. Happy sowing!

Journal 21 – Time Shall Be No More

> ***Revelation 10:6:*** *"And sware by him that liveth for ever and ever, who created heaven, and the things that therein are, and the earth, and the things that therein are, and the sea, and the things which are therein, that there should be time no longer."*

I find it good to pause, look over our lives, and see exactly what we are doing with our time. I understand as one man quoted, "We see going forward, but we learn looking backwards." Such powerful words of wisdom. The Word also says to consider your ways, think careful about something before you make decisions; it's safe to assume nothing.

Life can easily be so busy that we wonder where the time has gone. I am reminded of a song we used to sing that says you can count the years as months, the months as weeks, the weeks as days till He appears, it won't be long till Jesus comes. There are 365 days in a year, 24 hours in a day, 60 seconds in a minute, 28-31 days in a month, and 12 months in a year. Are we wasting time? If not, can we account for it? Let us be mindful of the time we have now and to frequently look back as well as forward and see where our lives truly stand with God.

I often contemplate many times before I go to sleep at night what my day was like, and I ask myself the following questions: Did I allow Christ to live in me? Did I do all that God would have expected me to do? Have I sinned or offended anyone? Did I

Time Shall Be No More

represent the Lord well? I simply go on to ask the Lord to forgive me because I don't know if I am going to wake up and see tomorrow. I want my heart to always be pure and right before Him. I believe we as a people take many things for granted, like waking up in the morning, or making it home after a day's work, but the truth is none of us know when we will be leaving this earth. That's why you should not put off tomorrow what can be done today because there may not be a tomorrow.

Today, let us allow God to strip search our hearts, motives, minds, and our entire lives. Let us also ask Him to come make needed adjustments in our lives, and remove all spiritual blindness and spiritual deafness that keeps us from hearing and seeing God clearly. We can't afford to be foolish or presumptuous. We only live once and may we live life without regrets. It's so easy for us to live our lives unto ourselves when in reality the life we now live is by faith in the Son of God and our lives are His to do as He chooses.

I see so many commercials on buying and storing food in case of a blackout, but are we investing in spiritual food for the days ahead? One thing I have come to know is if we are not in any type of a state of preparation, meaning spiritually, the chance of being caught off guard is inevitable. Think about it, most people buy life insurance policies to prepare for death. However, why do they become so lax in spiritual preparation on how to live to be prepared to stand before God, and expect to hear well done, but are

Awaken Oh Bride

likely to hear depart from me I never knew you. All preparations are done while we are here on earth to be prepared for the next life; it will be too late once we are gone from this life.

For instance, if we all stop now and look back at the day we first accepted Christ up to now, do our lives look totally transformed from who and what we used to be? Have we allowed Christ to live and remain in us, maturing and fashioning us into the man or woman He would have us to be? Are we more in love with Christ now than when we first accepted Him? Have our desires and love for the world changed? What about how much time we spend on leisurely activities such as ball games, vacations, summer camps, family fun, do we see our need for Him in those things? Furthermore, what about the things we watch on TV? Are the things we watch filled with sex, murder, violence, stealing, and lying? If so, we have to ask ourselves if Jesus walked in our homes and sat down with us would we be okay with Him watching it with us. These are serious things that need to be addressed. As I said from the onset of this journal it is meant to help awaken a people, which is my mandate from Christ. God is trying to awaken a people. Sin paralyzes. Sin kills and deadens us as a frog in a boiling pan of hot water. No kidding. This life is serious and time is short. We must not squander time.

The reality of what the Lord says either we are for Him or we are against Him. There is no gray area. We must stop letting the devil fool us and making us believe we have tomorrow to come to

Time Shall Be No More

Christ. We don't know that, and the minute we leave this earth, the life that we live will speak for us. We will all stand before the throne of God, be judged, and have to give an account of what we have done while here on earth. Did we allow Christ to grow in us, transform us, and allow Him to become our life? These are sober times and moments and we must **WAKE UP.** This is not a game. This life offers no do-overs. The way we live now will determine what Christ will say. Is what you are living for worth more than what Christ died for? Let us not answer too quickly. Selah!

Journal 22 – Chastened in the Love of God

Hebrews 12:6: "For whom the Lord loveth he chasteneth, and scourgeth every son whom he receiveth."

Just as our children can expect us to correct them, so we can expect the Lord to chasten (correct) us. To be chastened by Him means we are His sons and daughters. It means that God loves us. *Proverbs 3:11-12: "My son, despise not the chastening of the Lord; neither be weary of his correction. For whom the Lord loveth he correcteth; even as a father the son in whom he delighteth."* As long as we are here on earth, we will always be learning lessons. Some lessons we learn quickly. Other times not so quickly, but we must not give up or allow our heart to become hardened or discouraged when we are corrected by our Father. If we want to become disciples for Christ, then we must expect correction and become disciplined.

The Lord dropped in my spirit when I was studying this scripture that by obeying Him, we keep ourselves in the love of God. I was also reminded that the enemy's objective is to come between our relationships with our Father the same way He did with Eve in the garden. In Genesis 3:4-5, Eve received clear instructions from the Lord to not to eat from the tree in the midst of the garden. The enemy is very cunning and always waits for an open door such as the one he gained in Adam & Eve's life, for he knew if they ate of the tree, they would now know good and evil.

Chastened in the Love of God

However, the enemy also knew if they did eat the fruit, they would surely die. Therefore, their relationship and fellowship were broken with the Father and He had to chasten them by removing them from the garden.

As I mentioned earlier, we have a part to play in keeping ourselves in the love of God. ***John 14:21 says, "He that hath my commandments, and keepeth them, he it is that loveth me: and he that loveth me shall be loved of my Father, and I will love him, and will manifest myself to him."*** I am thankful that God loves us enough to chasten us, for Him not to would mean that we are bastards instead of sons and daughters. I am a witness that correction doesn't always feel good especially when you seem to have done your best and still missed the mark. In the end correction helps to mature us and lets us know we are loved by our Father.

We must go after God with our whole heart, mind, soul, and strength. We must love Him more than life itself and that comes with a price. Today, we must ask ourselves is the Lord worth it, is He worth every correction, is He worth me laying down my will, my thoughts, and my desires when He has other things in mind for me other than what I desire. That, my friends, is the real of it. I have experienced chastening over and over again, and it's both bitter and sweet. However, I came to understand no cross no crown.

Journal 23 – Disruption

> *Zephaniah 1:12 states, "And it shall come to pass at that time, that I will search Jerusalem with candles, and punish the men that are settled on their lees: that say in their heart, The LORD will not do good, neither will he do evil."*

We are currently living in an era of disruption. Disruption has come because God's people have settled on their laurels, thinking only Sunday service, and a Bible study class is enough. Sometimes we don't always realize we have settled and don't feel the need or urge to move forward. I have found it's usually in those times I have hit the brick wall and the Lord is calling me higher. Having been in that state before, in prayer the Lord told me that where I was in the current season of my life that I had gone as far as I could with Him from the plateau I was on. In order to progress and move up to the next level with my walk with Him, God said I had to allow His life to increase in me, by making adjustments to certain things in both my spiritual and physical life. If we are not progressing, we are regressing. There is no such thing as standing still. If we are not maturing spiritually, we will remain as spiritual babes never able to eat meat and move on to full maturity. We have to mature and be fit for the Master's use.

Therefore, the Lord is sending disruption that is meant to interrupt our patterns, such as ways of living, formulas, doctrines,

Disruption

theories, ways of thinking, activity, and inactivity. The Lord is concerned that we are involved and entangled in things and situations that are no longer moving us forward, but has us in a standing still mode in our desire for more of Him. Sometimes disruptions can be a situation that seems as though it's meant to destroy us, but it's only calling us back to the Father which is a place of progression. Because anytime we are not progressing we invite the enemy of status-quo. We have got to wake up and become firebrands (passionate people).

In Matthew 21:12 it says the day of disruption came the day Jesus walked in the temple and turned over the table of the money changers. The money changers had become comfortable with selling and cheating the poor, especially the widows, in the house of the Lord until the day of disruption came. Complacency is an enemy to the life of the believer. I have heard so many times it doesn't take all of that, yes it does and more if we are going to continue to go after God. Complacency moves us away from truths once established in our lives, in accordance with the Word of God. I am certain the money changers never thought they would be disrupted by Jesus as they were greedily buying and selling in the temple. However, complacency has a deadening effect on our hearts and lives. That day when Jesus walked in the temple things were uprooted. Like today, disruption has come and uprooted things in our lives, such as habits, sin, spiritual blindness, etc., to get our attention.

Awaken Oh Bride

We are living in times of great challenges that require us to keep our lamps full, filled up with God and in overflow status. Being full of God is Light and Life. Anytime we are not progressing we invite the enemy of status-quo. We are in a day of shaking unto an **AWAKENING** that leads to transformation as we continually behold the Lord. So, think it not strange if you are experiencing disruption in your life and allow the Lord to have His full work in you. He is making us, His Bride, ready to behold Him, the Lamb of God. It's a good day.

Journal 24 – Wimps vs. Warriors

When you hear the word war, what comes to mind . . . war on drugs, war on country borders, gang wars, and so many others? I now understand that war is a part of life and not just mere stories. In order to live in safe communities the reality is that some war is inevitable. *Ecclesiastes 3:8 tells us it's a time for war and a time for peace.* Today, I would like to awaken your spirit to the fact there is a time for war, and there is a war going on, and it is time for the Warrior inside of you and me to arise and conquer the evil that has overtaken our families, cities, nations, and schools.

Let's look at *1 Timothy 1:18-19: "This charge I commit unto thee, son Timothy, according to the prophecies which went before on thee, that thou by them mightest war a good warfare; Holding faith, and a good conscience; which some having put away concerning faith have made shipwreck."* The Apostle Timothy is telling us to war a good warfare. This charge leaves no room for excuses not to engage in war. The Bible is full of war stories of battles fought though not always won. However, Warriors must still arise, defeat, and prevail over the evil and all that resist God.

Let's take a look at two war stories in the Bible. One is in the book of Judges. The Lord sends Gideon to deliver Israel. Gideon was fearful because he said he was the least in his father's house.

Wimps vs. Warriors

The Lord encouraged him and told him I would be with thee and thou shalt smite the Midianites as one man **(See Judges 6:14-16)**. I can surely understand how Gideon felt. Sometimes things appear to be so overwhelming when we are looking from our view and not God's. I am a witness.

According to Judges Chapter 7, Israel was in battle against the Midianites, and the Lord told Gideon, the people that are with you are too many to go to battle, so the Lord had to reduce his army. Isn't it amazing that the Lord started with all those that were **FEARFUL** and **AFRAID—WIMPS**? Wimps are people who have no courage, and it's near impossible to fight without having courage. The enemy loves wimps because the warring spirit to fight has been neutralized because fear paralyzes. I believe the church needs to understand that the kingdom of darkness is very strategic. For ***Ephesians 6:12 states, "For we wrestle not against flesh and blood, but against principalities, against powers, against the rulers of the darkness of this world, against spiritual wickedness in high places."*** This demonic regiment is very orderly and works in sync with each other, and this scripture clearly shows the levels of their strategic armies. So, we must become strategic Warriors in our fighting.

For instance, I learned how to become a skillful Warrior in each battle I have fought using the weapons of my spiritual warfare to fight against the schemes of the enemy. ***Psalm 144:1 states,***

"Blessed be the LORD my strength, which teacheth my hands to war, and my fingers to fight." Honestly, it's the Lord that teaches us in war, and we can only learn as we stay engaged with the Lord in the battle. It's all victory from that standpoint.

Another war story in the Bible is that of David before he became king. David is an excellent example of a Warrior. He didn't just go to war one day and kill the giant Goliath, who was a Philistine. No! Let me explain by using ***1 Samuel 17:33-35: "And Saul said to David, Thou art not able to go against this Philistine to fight with him: for thou art but a youth, and he a man of war from his youth. And David said unto Saul, Thy servant kept his father's sheep, and there came a lion, and a bear, and took a lamb out of the flock: And I went out after him, and smote him, and delivered it out of his mouth: and when he arose against me, I caught him by his beard, and smote him, and slew him."*** The story begins while out in the field watching his father's sheep, David, as a young shepherd boy killed a lion and a bear to protect his father's flock. David won battles in the field while tending sheep because the Lord trains our hands to war while engaging in combat. As he became skillful and progressed in battle he also came to know and trust in his God. Indeed, it was neither by his power nor his might that he slew the bear and lion, but by the Spirit of the living God.

When Goliath was tormenting Saul and the Israelites, the scripture says they were dismayed and greatly afraid **(WIMPS)**,

so fearful that fear paralyzed them and they were too scared to fight Goliath. As the old folks used to say, God always has His own, and He had His own in the little shepherd boy, David. One day the **WARRIOR** David accepted the challenge to fight Goliath, and this is what happened that day. David hurled a stone from his sling and hit Goliath in the center of his forehead which killed him immediately. Therefore, the Israelites won the battle against the Philistine army. In the life of David, we continuously see the progression in his warfare, **(See 2 Samuel, Chapter 23 and 1 Chronicles, Chapter 11)**, which tells me the battles get no easier along the journey, but when the favor of God is on you your battles can be won. Because David was courageous, a worshipper of God, obedient and passionate to the Lord, he became a true Warrior for God's army.

Lord, help us not ever be afraid regardless of what type of fight we are facing and the many ugly faces it shows. Some are faces of sickness and disease, loneliness, hurt, pain, financial disasters, spiritual, etc. Whatever battle you are in today, be encouraged, stand up, and fight. David has shown us what type of Warrior we can become if we are courageous. There are some things today I am confident the Lord has for you, but you will have to fight for them. Issues and problems can be stubborn at times and refuse to move; sometimes they can wear you down. But be encouraged, you can fight, and you can win. Stand with the sword

of the Lord in your right hand. Let the kingdom of darkness know that there is a name that is above every name. His name is Jesus and every problem, issue, sickness, or whatever must bow to His name. The battle that you're in now is preparing you for your next one when you, like David, will face your Goliath.

Who is the greatest of all Warriors? ***Revelation 5:5 states, "And one of the elder's saith unto me, Weep not: behold, the Lion of the tribe of Juda, the Root of David, hath prevailed to open the book, and to loose the seven seals thereof."*** All through the Word we can see the Lion of the tribe of Judah in action forever fighting, forever conquering, and forever overcoming. We are in a progression to become overcomers. As the Word says they that overcome shall reign with Him. We overcome by the blood of the lamb, the word of our testimony, and if we are born of God, we overcome by war for nothing will be handed to us. Remember, we are born to fight and to win.

Could it be that you too are like David facing a Goliath in your life? However, let me encourage you to fear not, look the enemy in the face and remember the Lion of the Tribe of Judah lives within. Let Him roar, let Him loose to stand and fight for the victory is already won, **WARRIOR!**

Journal 25 – Suffering

So, how is your day? Are you having one of those days we call a bad day because it seems any and everything that could go wrong is going wrong? Not only going wrong today but has been for quite a while. Don't think it strange; you're actually in the right place. *1 Peter 4:11-12 says, "Beloved, think it not strange concerning the fiery trial which is to try you, as though some strange thing happened unto you: But rejoice, because ye are partakers of Christ's sufferings; that, when his Glory shall be revealed, ye may be glad also with exceeding joy."* I understand if you may not see it that way, neither did I. It seemed my pain and suffering spoke louder than the Word of God. I became conformed to old patterns and belief systems that led me to believe trouble is never good and only brings pain. I depended heavily on teachings that said I could confess my way out of stuff and that I had power over the enemy, and I needed to take authority and get the victory. I realize some things and situations in our lives have to run their course regardless of the pain. The test will work for our good, and we gain power through victory, such as the cross.

Earlier in my life, I used to feel as though something was wrong with me even after having doing all the religious confession ceremonies, something was still wrong with me. I had issues in my health, my job, my finances, relationships, and so much more. As I studied the Word and became mature in some areas of my life, the Lord unveiled truths that I could not see, nor could I understand at

Suffering

one time. I have found that God's Word is to be meat, chewed (applied), and digested; milk will not bring about the results in our spiritual maturity to discern and understand the Word of God. Regardless of how much we can confess it, milk is for babes in Christ. Milk gets us started as we progress on to the meat.

Because we are partakers of Christ and His divine nature, we are automatically candidates for the sufferings of Christ, and it says we ought to REJOICE! We can rejoice because Christ's Glory will shine in us. Think back to how many of our songs are regarding send your Glory Lord; we want to see your Glory, right? Our carnal minded has made us believe Glory only has to do with seeing God move in healings, signs, and wonders or in a church service. Instead, suffering brings about the Glory of God. The church has become adapted to what I call the Sugar Gospel, and everything is always about the good, the blessings, me, and everything else. Unfortunately, we have a problem handling the real Glory, **SUFFERING,** which is sad because suffering is necessary for our growth and maturity in Christ. Many times, I have studied and read about the lives of the twelve Apostles and was blessed by their love and commitment to Christ, how great their ministries were. Many times, I look at their life stories which have encouraged me and say to myself I want to live for God and be an example such as the Apostles. However, after studying their lives, I see the price they each paid for greatness, which allowed

the life of Christ to be transformed in and through them. It's astounding how much they all suffered for the cause of Christ.

Let's briefly look at the twelve Apostles and how they died. It is eye-opening, something to be aware of in our journey. The lives of the Apostles leave a sober reality of the price others have paid compared to our minor sufferings.

In Matthew 14:10, John was in prison and beheaded. In Acts 7:59, Stephen was stoned as he kneeled and cried out with a loud voice. They killed James with the sword in Acts 12:2. All I can say is my God, they paid the ultimate price, and we find them all in the Word of God as a testimony of Glory through their suffering. I often hear a lot of the blessed good life preaching but very little about suffering that the Glory comes through pain. Most so-called Apostles speak very little of suffering, and the price paid for the representation of Christ. Something is wrong if everything is always sweet, pleasant, peaceful, and safe without conflict. Most prophetic words that I hear spoken are towards people, but rarely if ever, are about the testimony of Christ. As I progressed in my journey moving from milk to meat, the Lord opened my eyes through His Word for the understanding of suffering and how it would work out for my good. We see in *1 Peter 5:10: "But the God of all grace, who hath called us unto his eternal Glory by Christ Jesus, after that ye have suffered a while, make you perfect, stablish, strengthen, settle you."* It's impossible to

Suffering

separate Glory from suffering. Look at all that suffering does for us. It perfects us. It establishes us. It strengthens us and settles us. Look at the growth that comes through suffering in Christ. It won't matter what happens because it will establish us in Christ just as the Apostles were established. It established them unto death. They refused to deny Christ, and we now are reading about their Apostleship because they remained in Christ and were not moved. Paul spoke about what persecutions he endured; but out of them all the Lord delivered them **(See 2 Timothy 3:11),** and so He will do for us.

Saints, it's time we open up the Word and our hearts to Christ that He might reveal to us the truth of His Word. So much of the easy way is preached that most will not be ready to suffer persecution when it comes. As we read to become established, we must stay in the trial, and suffer to allow God's Glory and work to be complete in us. The way is difficult and not meant to be easy. We are in the process of being prepared for the final battle. I encourage you to open the Word for yourself and ask the Holy Spirit to teach you in the scriptures. The feel-good gospel doesn't require much of us. The way of the cross is about suffering, and as we read the Apostles died for what they believed.

As I have said many times, we are living in the latter times, dangerous times, and I have penned this journal for that reason. I also stated at the beginning of this journal that the Lord told me He is trying to **AWAKEN** a people, and He said awaken means **A**

WAY OUT. A way out of what I thought I knew, a way out of old patterns and lifestyles, a way out of blindness and deception into a whole-hearted relationship in God. Christ has made a way out for us to return to Him in repentance. God is relational though He is many times presented to be a Jesus Santa Claus as though He's only here to bless us and give us what we want and saying yes to all of our requests. I'm sorry that is not the case. We need a real encounter from God, one that first starts internal that affects the external. Time is short. The Lord said I will not always strive with man. We must take advantage of our windows of opportunity.

May you be blessed today, and whatever suffering you may have to endure remain. Let that suffering establish you, perfect you, and make you whole, wanting nothing. He will deliver you. I'm a living witness.

Journal 26 – Desperation

Can you imagine being lost in the desert, the temperature is well over a hundred degrees; you are hot, sweaty, and weak and to complicate the matter, have very little water left? You realize that finding water has become more critical than immediately finding your way out. ***Psalm 42:1-2,*** which is one of my favorite scriptures, says, ***"As the hart panteth after the water brooks, so pantheth my soul after thee, O God."*** The nature of deer is to pant for water because of their lack of sweat glands for survival. They must find water to live. ***Psalm 63:8 says, "My soul follows hard after thee."*** This scripture says it all; everything within us must crave and be drawn by Him. Life at times can become a long journey; we grow weary, but in no wise can give up. We are on a journey to meet our King. Long trips, if not careful, can cause us to lose our focus, and we slowly become lax or lukewarm.

So, if perhaps you feel that today, let me awaken you and tell you to arise and be as the deer. I have come to know how desperately I need Christ. I do not believe that the church as a whole realizes how desperately we need God. In the book of ***Revelation 3:14-18,*** the church of Laodiceans was the last church the Lord spoke to, and they were told you say they are rich, increased with good, and have need of nothing. The Lord said in His Word when you seek me with all your heart you will find me. We can never become self-sufficient as the Laodiceans did.

Desperation

One night I had a dream that I was living out in the wilderness. All of a sudden, I saw these men begin to dump a lot of dead deer one after the other in heaps and piles. The piles of deer had become high and there were too many to count. Suddenly, I cried out to those that were dumping the deer and said, "We almost do not have any more space for dumping; please don't dump anymore deer out here." Upon waking, I sat before the Lord and meditated the meaning of the dream. The Lord explained to me that the deer had quit panting for water and died out in the wilderness. He went on to say this is what is happening to people; they are no longer panting after me.

Consequently, along our journey of life, if we begin to no longer thirst for righteousness and desire for Christ, as the deer, we will eventually die out for lack of longing and passion for Him. My God, the profound and sad reality of that is as a church we have to be careful about what we are panting and longing after. I hear a lot of people talking about I'm running after my destiny, I'm getting mine, I'm this, and I'm that. If the truth is told, Christ never told us to run after those things, He said to seek Him, and **EVERYTHING ELSE WOULD BE ADDED.**

Conversely, let me put a bug in your ear today; it is the trick of the enemy to get us to pant and run after everything but God. It's time to become as the hart and begin to pant after Christ, the living water; to ask Christ to draw us that we become not faint and die in the wilderness of this journey of life. Think about it, Jesus came

Awaken Oh Bride

saying I came to do the will of my Father; never did He ever come to set up His own Kingdom though He knew He was the Messiah. He came knowing He would decrease as His Father increased. The scripture indicates God, His Father, was given the glory at the end of His story, not man! What about us? Don't faint, Christ the living water is present. *Selah!*

Journal 27 – Doors

Doors! How many have you walked through today or even over the course of your life? Not just physical doors but spiritual doors. I can testify that I have walked through many doors over the course of my life and some I walked through I wished I had slammed shut. Nonetheless, the Lord said that He set an open door when speaking to the Philadelphia church **(See Revelation 3:8)**, so this gives us indication that the Lord does open doors that no man can shut.

In the book of ***Proverbs 8:34, it reads, "Blessed is the man that heareth me, watching daily at my gates, waiting at the post of my doors."*** Watching means to be alert, to be on the lookout. When we rise each day, He knows all that we will encounter, and if we are watching at His doors, He will give us direction and instructions for the day. When we are waiting at His doors, it is an entrance way, into His understanding, into His wisdom, and into His spiritual truths. I come to find and understand the importance of waiting daily at the Lord's gates. When we wait on the Lord at His gates, He is protecting us from what could possibly be unseen dangers as well as guarding and protecting us so that we may receive all that He has for us. I think that is so beautiful and it works. One morning, while waiting at the door, the Lord spoke something else to me in reference to me regarding doors that brought so much reality to me. It was a WOW moment. **(See Matthew 25:1-13)** This is a parable of the ten virgins. The five foolish virgins were not prepared as they did not take enough oil with them and the five wise virgins told them to go to those that sell because it wasn't enough for both of them. While they were gone, the bridegroom arrived and those who were ready went in to meet Him. When the foolish returned, the **DOOR** was shut. My God, I can't imagine.

As I continued to read and meditate the Lord said to me it will be necessary for my people to be watching for me daily at my **DOORS** in order to be ready to walk through my open **DOOR** on my return. To all of us He will either say well done thy good and faithful servant or depart from me ye that work iniquity, I know you not. That is so frightening to me, and beyond my mental comprehension to grasp the totality and reality of being separated from the Lord forever. My God, we can't be like the foolish virgins.

Today my brothers and sisters, we will each decide if Christ is worth it, if He's worth the wait. I encourage you to choose wisely for **there's only one DOOR called the WAY, THE TRUTH, and THE LIFE.** The trumpet is sounding. *Selah!*

Journal 28 – The Price Is the Same

Once again while waiting on the Lord in prayer I heard the Lord whisper, "The hour is late. The penny a day worker has showed up." I knew the story He was referring to but of course, I had to further study and ask for understanding and clarity as to what exactly He was saying to me. The Lord brought me to the book of Matthew, Chapter 20, verses 1-16, where I read of an owner of an estate who went out to hire workers to work in his vineyard. Before sending them out, the workers agreed with the owner to work for a penny a day. After hiring the early workers, he saw others standing idle in the marketplace, hired them to work after they also agreed for a penny a day. At about the last hour of the day, five o'clock in the evening, he hired the last group of workers and they also agreed to work for a penny a day. At the end of the day when it was time to pay the workers, the owner paid them beginning from the last unto the first. When the first that were hired were paid, they thought they should have received more because they had worked all day, but they received a penny as they agreed. The workers began to grumble and complain against the owner. The owner immediately answered one of them and said, "Friend, do thee no wrong; did we not agree on a penny and I can do what I will with my own?"

As I said earlier, man does not see as God sees. The Lord, when further explaining what He was trying to convey to me in reference to the phrase, He spoke the penny a day workers have

The Price Is the Same

showed up. I understood Him saying here is a shift going on, there have been some that have been sent first to work in the Lord's vineyard but have gone their way, as it was most about themselves, money, name, fame, or whatever. The Word says the last shall be first, and the first last.

As I went on to meditate, the Lord said it doesn't matter when someone decides to come follow me, the price is still the same. As the price was the same for all workers, so the price Christ paid on the cross is for everyone. He's an all or nothing God that we can't bargain with as the workers tried to bargain with the owner of the vineyard. Be Blessed! And spend your penny wisely.

Journal 29 – Capturing the Heart of the King

There is a narrative in the Old Testament in the book of Esther about a king named Xerxes who seeks and marries (Esther) a new wife after his queen, Vashti, refuses to obey him. King Xerxes is captivated by Esther's beauty, and she captures his heart. Once Queen Esther captures King Xerxes' heart, she obtains entrance into all that the King has and it brings her to a whole new place, both spiritually and physically. The life she had formerly lived and known had all vanished. Everything changed. She went from living in the outer chambers of the palace into the inner rooms. Oh, how this depicts the life of a Christian as we progress in our relationship with our King. As we become His friend, He reveals His secrets and unveils a part of His nature only in the secret place. When Saints gather on Sunday, we come to meet and worship Christ our King corporately, but what He does corporately will not compare to what He does personally with us because He is relational. That is why He is our **personal Lord and Savior,** and I love it!

Therefore, in these end times, it will be what I call Lovers of the Bridegroom. Lovers of the groom are only going after Christ, the Lamb of God, and nothing else. They have passed the elementary place of asking for blessings, names, and titles because they realize God has an eternal purpose, and we are His inheritance. Everything that will challenge their love will lose their power because they know that His love is stronger than death. The Lord proved that love was more potent than death when He died on the cross because death could not hold Him down. Lovers of the Bridegroom realize to die is to gain, and none can compare. They have come to the reality that whatever they have to go through to reach His heart is worth it all—every hurt, every denial, every pain. As the Word says now that I have found the one my soul loves, I will not let Him go! Amen.

As a result, Lovers of the Bridegroom have become captivated by the love of their King and will not compromise and give way to all that the enemy flashes as temptations. They know that Christ is the treasure, and they are rich in Him. By His captivation, the King knows He is no longer concerned about other lovers taking His place as He is sufficient in all things that pertain unto life and godliness in the presence of His Bride. His Bride that He will so come back for as she makes herself ready.

Pure love and passion for the Bridegroom is the order of the day in these end times. We rise to live and love the groom. We grow to hasten the coming of the King. Love for the Bridegroom is the fuel needed to conquer everyday battles; the fuel required for us to pursue the one we love. We must come to fear to be lukewarm in our love for Christ. As Christ told the church of Ephesus in *Revelation 2:2: I know thy works, and thy labour, and thy patience, and how thou canst not bear them which are evil: and thou hast tried them which say they are apostles, and are not, and hast found them liars."* He also says in *Revelation 2:4-5:* "*Nevertheless I have somewhat against thee because thou have*

left thy first love. Remember therefore whence thou are fallen, and repent, and do the first works; or else I will come unto thee quickly, and will remove thy candlestick out of his place, except thou repent." My God, help us. It is a journey of submission, and obedience birthed out of love for our Master.

In conclusion, may we allow Christ to examine our hearts today and send the purging fire and the spirit of repentance which the church so severely lacks? We must repent and ask the King to teach us how to love Him with our whole heart. Much of the church today is in a cold place, loving gifts, signs, wonders, names and titles, but lacking the maturity of Christ. It's time we get back to the basics and love Him for who He is and what He has to give. The trumpet is being sounded today for those that have ears to hear. The hour is late, and we need adjustments in our lives. We must allow Christ to become everything to us. We must become captivated by the beauty and love of our King. The King is awaiting our arrival. Will you rise and meet Him? I will.

Journal 30 – KISS

KISS, for the sake of those that do not know, stands for Keep It Simple Stupid! The acronym KISS was used as a design principle initiated by a military group in 1960. So, please do not take it personally, I am not calling you stupid.

Oh, the simplicity of the Garden of Eden in which Adam and Eve walked with God in the cool of the day without toil or strain just living in fellowship with their Creator and one another. Simply beautiful! KISS! They lived a simple life until the day they sinned, and God banished them from the garden. However, from that day forth, they had to work and till the ground to eat, which is something God never intended for us.

Our first calling is to be with Him. ***Mark 3:14 says***, ***"And he ordained twelve, that they <u>should be with him</u>, and that he might send them forth to preach."*** Our relationship at one time was carefree without toil and the simplicity of simply knowing Christ and being with Him has been lost. ***2 Corinthians 11:3 says, "But I fear, lest by any means, as the serpent beguiled Eve through his subtilty, so your minds should be corrupted from the simplicity that is in Christ."***

However, I have found it takes man to muddy the water and complicate anything when Christ has made it so simple. KISS! Since He says come follow, take no thought for your life, seek ye first the kingdom and everything will be added, give and it shall be given; I hope you get the picture. For instance, when He chose the twelve disciples He did not find them in perfect conditions, yet He knew their needs, wants and desires, but simply said come follow me. The come follow me is an indication that He would be to them everything they needed, and they did not have to look any further. Christ wanted to be with them, and did not choose them for what they could do for Him or give Him. Our love and relationship with Christ is about singleness of heart and **pure devotion.** Please understand that **pure devotion** does not come out of producing works, ministry, or anything else. At some point, we must come to embrace the reality that we should value all things to the price of what they will gain in eternity. Much of what we do and have does not presently have any eternal value, but rather boosts our ego. It's so easy to do things because of the validation it may bring us in the light of the world or even how it makes us feel. May the Lord help us to be careful and do all things as unto the Lord. KISS!

Let's look at the story of Mary and Martha which gives great clarification and examples of the outcomes of what happens when we choose to go the way of simplicity just being with Christ or we choose to go the way of works, to produce something for Christ. *Luke 10:40-42 reads, "But Martha was cumbered about much serving, and came to him, and said, Lord, dost thou not care that my sister hath left me to serve alone? bid her therefore that she help me. And Jesus answered and said unto her, Martha, Martha, thou art careful and troubled about many things: But*

one thing is needful: and Mary hath chosen that good part, which shall not be taken away from her."

It looks like that day Mary said I am not worrying about anything, Jesus is coming and I just want to be with Him. Whatever I need, He is well able to perform it, and I mean He works miracles all the time. Martha, who I can understand was worrying about being hospitable that day to Jesus, but it was burdensome for her because she thought Mary should have been helping her. Somehow, some people of God like Martha have been lured into working to produce things to offer God or do for Him. They are involved in so many activities, such as committees, mission groups for trips, bake sales, garage sales, this team, etc., that simply keep them from communing and fellowshipping with God. KISS!

This also reminds me of the church committee call, or the food pantry call, or the selling chicken dinner call, all in the name of Jesus. Oh! But I love what the Lord said to Mary, she has chosen that good part which shall not be taken away from her. That good part of spending time with the Father, that simple relationship part is that Christ is imparting Himself unto her, cannot be taken away. Everything that is of this world will pass away; only that which is eternal will last. KISS!

One day while praying and talking with the Lord He spoke to me and said busyness leads to carelessness. I thought wow! When we become so busy in our so-called working for God, which leads

to busyness, we become careless or negligent and things start to slip in our devotedness to Him. Christ never created us to work for Him, but to be with Him. He is a God of relationship. Eventually busyness will push Christ from being Alpha (number one) in our daily lives because we don't find time in our busy schedules to fit Him in. Oh, if we can remember the beauty of the garden, the simplicity of just being with Christ because we love Him, and not because we are compelled to work for Him. I encourage you today before you become as Martha, make sure you can spiritually afford to spend time in prayer and in the Word with the Father so you won't lose the good part. *KISS and Selah*!

Journal 31 – What Type of Lover Are You?

In these end times there will be two kinds of lovers, Lovers of the Bridegroom and Lovers of Self. Lovers of the Bridegroom are only going after Christ and nothing else. As the Song of Solomon says and so will the lover of the Bridegroom say now that I have found the one my soul loveth, I will not let Him go. **(See Song of Solomon 3:4).** I have discovered that when I found the one my soul loves, I became complete, and all that I needed and desired was in Him. In this journey I've realized the things that I once thought I desired and wanted, I no longer needed because I became complete in Him. *As Solomon 2:4 says, "His banner over me is love."* This banner of protection, love, meets the standard that nothing is greater than Him. I now understand the song I used to sing as a little girl about loving Jesus because He first loved me. Jesus proved His love for you and me by giving up His life and dying for us, truly there is no greater love. Love is all about a laid down life.

In contrast, the Lovers of Self are a life full of self reliance, self-energy, self-interest, self-effort, self-focus, self-life, and self-desires. Self, if not careful, will cause us to self-destruct; because the Word says apart from me you can do nothing. We can do nothing because we are separated from Christ when we are the self-lover. During these end times the church must stop running after other lovers and be joined with the Bridegroom.

What Type of Lover Are You?

The scripture tells us no man can serve two masters **(See Luke 16:13)** regardless of what other master we serve, be it money, ourselves, or others. Christ will only give Himself to those who willfully give themselves to Him in full commitment of love and dedication. He is looking for vessels that He can inhabit in such a way that will allow all of Him to come through in the fullness of all He is, but we must become Lovers of the Bridegroom.

We are approaching a wedding day and we must allow our groom to make us ready. He wants to put His ring on our hand and write His name on our forehead, but it's one thing that stands between us and Him and that is SELF. Can we let go of self to all our desires, aspirations, hopes, and destinies to realize He is our destiny and not becoming something in and of ourselves?

May today be a new day of love and commitment to the one we love, our heavenly Father. Lord, today we ask that you teach us how to love you as we love one another. Amen

Journal 32 – Wait! Gingerbread Man

Isaiah 40:31: *"But they that wait upon the Lord shall renew their strength; they shall mount up with wings as eagles; they shall run, and not be weary, and they shall walk, and not faint."*

I am sure most of us as children grew up hearing or reading the story of the gingerbread man. He gave the little baker lady a run for her life. Once she had cooked him and opened up the oven door to take him out, Poof! Out he went chanting run, run as fast as you can, you can't catch me, I'm the gingerbread man. Boy, don't I know that story. When the Lord opens up the oven door of life's circumstances in my life for my good, many times I have taken out running. The furnace of affliction is part of the process where we become complete and mature. It's merely a part of the works and doings of God. *Isaiah 48:10 says, "Behold I have refined thee but not with silver; I have chosen thee in the furnace of affliction".* Fire both refines and purifies us of self-toxins, sin-toxins, and all else that defiles us. The Word of God says He is coming back for a bride without spot, wrinkle, or blemish. With that in mind, I understand why we encounter tests and trials along our journey in life. Having come through the furnace a few times, I came to realize the furnace was not for my destruction but construction.

The gingerbread man is an excellent example of what happens when we don't wait to go through the refining process because

refining helps prepare us for what God has for us. Whenever trusting myself, the outcome was not favorable, and I learned being unwilling to go through the process is never good. Anytime we refuse to wait and not go through the process we will lack in all that is needed to keep us on our journey or place of ministry where Christ has called us.

I refer back to a scripture that says if you wait on the Lord he renews our strength and we will mount up with wings as eagles, because I will be the first to say waiting is so hard but necessary. All throughout the scripture people waited on the Lord and it's no different for us if we are going to do it God's way and not ours. The disciples waited in the upper room; no doubt not being prepared totally for what was to come. Jesus was led up in the wilderness and was tested. The Lord instructed Abraham to move away from his kindred. In every one of those situations, there was a period of waiting.

I urge you today if you are in a period of waiting and in the furnace of affliction—wait! Don't run like the gingerbread man. In your waiting draw near to God and let Him finish and complete His process in you. It will be worth it. The reality is if walking with God was easy, everybody would be doing it, and doing it God's way.

In these end times and days, Christ is maturing His Bride, and conflict, battle, and challenges are a part of that maturing. Our love for the Lamb of God must and will be proven. The secret is in

Awaken Oh Bride

waiting. When we wait we will mount up with wings as eagles. Eagles fly above the storm and fly alone. Eagles can see all that is below, which gives them the advantage. I encourage you today to wait patiently in the oven while Christ is being formed in you. I know it's hot, but we both know Hell is hotter. LOL! Have an awesome day.

Journal 33 – Get Out of the Ness!

Baby birds are called fledglings until they are about 13-14 days old. They are fully feathered and are able to hop and walk though at that time may not be good fliers. However, the fledgling is able to leave the nest! I am reminded of what the Apostle Paul said in *1 Corinthians 3:2*: *"I have fed you with milk, and not with meat: for hitherto ye were not able to bear it, neither yet now are ye able."* This scripture gives clear indications that the saints should have matured and been able to eat meat and not have to drink milk at that time. They should have been out of the nest and flown on their way to maturity. If not careful, the nest can become a comfortable place for us, meaning it is familiar to us and we know what to expect. It becomes a place of comfort too long. If the fledgling never becomes able to hop, which leads to flying, their growth will become inhibited because the nest will have become too small. What once was a place of safety now has become a place that is hazardous. The Word of God speaks a lot about some of the hazards of NESS!

Laziness is dangerous to our maturing in Christ; you cannot be lazy and go after God at the same time. It takes effort to push your way out of a Ness into maturity. One of the best stories about laziness is the story of the ten talents **(See Matthew 25)**. The master gave each of his servants' talents. To one he gave five talents, to another two, and he gave one to another. However, to the one he gave one talent to, did nothing with the talent to bring

Get Out of the Ness!

increase to his master while his master was gone. The master on his return noted in **Matthew 25:26-27: *"His lord answered and said unto him, Thou wicked and slothful servant, thou knewest that I reap where I sowed not, and gather where I have not strawed: Thou oughtest therefore to have put my money to the exchangers, and then at my coming I should have received mine own with usury."*** We find here that laziness cost the servant eternal life, as it will do the same for us. **Proverbs 13:4: *"The soul of the sluggard desireth, and hath nothing: but the soul of the diligent shall be made fat."*** I heard someone once say, "Each of us have as little or much of God as we want, and I couldn't agree more. Today we each decide if we will crawl out of the Ness of laziness!

Another Ness we want to crawl out of is Stubbornness. All through the Old Testament we find stubbornness and how it cost the children of Israel and many others from being blessed. Among them was King Saul who was rebellious to the Word of the Lord and the Lord rejected him from being King of Israel. Let's look at **1 Samuel 15:23: *For rebellion is as the sin of witchcraft, and stubbornness is as iniquity and idolatry. Because thou hast rejected the word of the LORD, he hath also rejected thee from being king.*** I am certain King Saul never saw the day coming of his removal from being King due to his rebellion against God. Although God is a merciful God, King Saul must have forgotten God is still a God of judgment. Nowadays you hear so much about

Awaken Oh Bride

God being a God of blessings, and He is. However, we must remember He is also a God of judgment, and He will judge in His time. We must never become comfortable in sin and see it as God does. He abhors it and so should we. The Bible speaks of a cup of iniquity meaning our actions are being weighed and judgment will be set if we are a people that will continue to be stubborn against the Lord and His ways. Let us consider our ways, repent for God is a God of great mercy but He is also a God of great judgment because He loves us as a Father.

The next Ness we must crawl from, though there are many Nesses, is Sinfulness. I am certain we all know what sin is and its danger to our lives. To put it plain and blunt SIN KILLS period. King David, in the book of Psalms, prayed often about sin, as we should. **Psalm 31:10: "Indeed, my life is consumed with grief and my years with groaning; my strength has failed because of my sinfulness, and my bones waste away."** Sin destroys our lives. Let us allow the resurrected life of Christ to live through us. It was the resurrection power of Christ, that removed the grave clothes from Lazarus, and that power will do the same for us. Sin is merely grave clothes that bandage us up and put us in bondage that leads to death. Thank God Christ lives, and He is alive in us. Today let us allow God to arise and His enemies in us to be destroyed.

As we proceed from crawling out of the Ness and on our way of becoming mature, let us be careful of the Ness of Busyness. We cannot afford to be busybodies in others' business as the Bible says

but let us be busy going after God. The old folks used to say idle time is the devil's workshop and I found that to be true. Let us make the most of our time doing good and going hard in the paint after God. I pray that today's journal helped in some way, and remember no matter where you are in your journey you can continue or start again. Remember the idle workers that stood outside to work in the vineyard? The penny a day worker had a great ending. So will you, just remember to stay out of the NESS! God loves you and so do I. We are in this thing together, this journey called life. We may not be perfect, but we are on our way to allowing Christ the perfected one to be perfected in us. The key is as long as our hearts are perfect toward God, we can make it with His help. Be blessed!

Journal 34 – Safe on Home Plate

Although I have never been a big softball or baseball fan, I was required to play it in PE in Junior High School. What I remembered and liked most about the game was hearing the Referee say s-a-f-e after the runner made it to home plate.

How wonderful it would be if it was that easy for us after we accepted Christ as our Savior and to say safe, I'm home and on my way to heaven. Though it is true once we accept Christ we are "saved" but not safely home yet. In **Philippians 2:12, it says, *"Wherefore, my beloved, as ye have always obeyed, not as in my presence only, but now much more in my absence, work out your own salvation with fear and trembling."***

No doubt we should have a constant alarm about working out our own salvation until we leave here, for there is no home safe base. Upon studying I found the Greek word for fear is alarm, isn't that interesting? If we are not careful over time, we can become complacent in our journey with the Lord as this race is long distance and not a hundred-yard dash. The Lord gave a warning to His people, woe to them that are at ease in Zion **(See Amos 6:1)**. The Greek words for ease are security and haughty. To be at ease is to be complacent or comfortable with the current state of things. I find when everything is going well is when it's easy to become secure and it seems there is no need for anything, but nothing can be further from the truth. That ease should alarm us and the fear of

working out our own salvation in fear and trembling should arise all the more.

Therefore, we now stand with a chance to swing the bat just as the players at the softball game. Each swing in our journey in pursuing God must be with the goal of reaching home plate safely. Our salvation that Christ brought through the triumph of the cross must be worked out in fear and trembling. If we are to reach the home plate of heaven to avoid the fear of missing Christ, we should try not striking out at the batter's plate. We cannot allow strikeouts in our lives by loving the game of life more than we love God. Let us be alarmed today!

So, remember, the next time someone says once saved always saved tell them NO, we must work out our own salvation in fear and trembling. The completion of our salvation is when we reach the home plate of heaven. If you or I think we are going to slide into heaven on home plate without a fight, something is wrong. Batter, batter swing, hit it out of the park, and run until you reach the home plate of heaven.

Journal 35 – Let's Keep It Real! Hell Is Real

Have you ever had a bad nightmare or a dream that was so real? When you finally awakened, were you glad that it was only a dream? I have, many times. In this journal, I want to talk about a nightmare that is real which we'll never awake from, and that's a place called Hell. The Bible speaks of Hell being a real place, as we can see in *2 Peter 2:4: "For if God spared not the angels that sinned, but cast them down to Hell, and delivered them into chains of darkness, to be reserved unto judgment."* Another reference is found in *Matthew 13:4: "And shall cast them into a furnace of fire: there shall be wailing and gnashing of teeth."* Because the Lord sent His Son Jesus Christ to die for our sins, we no longer are doomed to this place called Hell. Though we are not doomed, we can choose to go by our own free will. One might ask, "Well, why or how would I decide to go to that dreadful place?" I agree, but our decision and manner of life will choose for us.

For instance, the Lord, in His goodness, left guidelines in His Word on how to live and spend an eternity with Him. The Bible declares in *Matthew 7:21-23: "Not everyone that saith unto me, Lord, Lord, shall enter into the kingdom of heaven; but he that doeth the will of my Father which is in heaven. Many will say to me in that day, Lord, Lord, have we not prophesied in thy name? and in thy name have cast out devils? and in thy name done many wonderful works? And then will I profess unto them, I never knew you: depart from me, ye that work iniquity. It is he that doeth the will of the Father that enters into heaven and not us going our way and doing what we want. Only doing works for God will not be enough, as we can see from scripture. When we keep God's commandments, his holy word, it means that we love him."*

Furthermore, the warning in Galatians tells what happens if we do not keep His Word and allow the works of the flesh to become our lifestyle. The works of the flesh are what will send us directly to the pits of Hell. Let's read **Galatians 5:19-25:** *"Now the works of the flesh are manifest, which are these; Adultery, fornication, uncleanness, lasciviousness. Idolatry, witchcraft, hatred, variance, emulations, wrath, strife, seditions, heresies. Envyings, murders, drunkenness, revellings, and such like: of the which I tell you before, as I have also told you in time past, that they which do such things shall not inherit the kingdom of God."*

Hence, I urge you today if you find yourself in this list to pray and ask the Lord for His strength and forgiveness before it's too late. The spirit of conviction, which is the Holy Spirit, convicts our hearts of sin. If our hearts do not sense the conviction of sin, something is wrong. None of us knows the minute or the moment we will leave this earth, and we can't afford to assume we have time.

Furthermore, I have found the devil to be masterful in deception. He is prolific in trickery and makes what's dark appear

Awaken Oh Bride

as light, evil as good, and a lie for the truth. As the Word says, we cannot be ignorant of the enemy's devices. Satan, the devil, would make us believe that sin is not a big deal and all we have to do is ask God for forgiveness. Yes, there is some truth in that, but the truth is willful sinning will separate us from God's love, joy, and peace. ***Hebrews 10:26-27 says, "For if we sin willfully after that, we have received the knowledge of the truth, there remaineth no more sacrifice for sins, but a certain fearful looking for of judgment and fiery indignation, which shall devour the adversaries."***

If there was ever a time to take sin, hell and judgment seriously, it is now. In everyday life, we purchase insurance policies to make sure we are taken care of when we leave this earth. How about our eternal spiritual lives? Being a doer of the Word of God is our policy for life; it covers us for when we leave this earth. Heaven is our home, and we must prepare to go there. Preparation takes time. Awaken, and start preparing today as tomorrow may not come.

Only you and I individually will decide where we will spend eternity. Each day by our decisions, we are judging. Will we choose heaven, or will we choose hell? From the beginning, after the fall of Satan, Hell was created for Satan and his angels and not Christians, so why choose Hell? Christ is eternal life; may we choose life and live.

Journal 36 – Will God Be Enough?

Often, I had imagined what it must have been like for the children in the wilderness when they came to the Red Sea, and Pharaoh's army was behind them chasing them down while they were facing the Red Sea. I am more than confident that was a frightening experience though many times they had seen God work miracle after miracle for them. I, for one, understand that sometimes things that we see can become more significant than the God we know. Situations only become more prominent than the God we know if He has not become enough and all that we need. I one day realized regardless of the outcome of any situation, test or trial, He is and will always be God. It is so easy to speak and agree with something when you are not down in a foxhole fighting for your life and confronted to work out everything you believe and to prove your trust in God. My reality is will God be enough for me as He was for them or for Job? Will my allegiance and confidence in God remain in the evil day, or will my loyalty align with man or what I see and what I feel? Job, as we know, was perfect and upright in God's sight, one that feared God, and eschewed evil.

At one time, I was so perplexed when I read this story because I thought why is all this bad stuff happening to Job when he was a righteous man? Though I now understand that we all at some point in our lives will be tried and tested in our love, and prove our allegiance to the God we love or say we love. We are all on a journey of testing, as we are making preparations to meet the King.

Will God Be Enough?

For Job, it seemed when it rained, it poured. He had one personal disaster after another while serving God. He lost all his oxen, his servants slain, fire fell from heaven, burned up his sheep, and consumed them. I am sure, at one point, he thought it could not get any worse. His sons and daughters were eating, drinking, and a high wind came and destroyed the house they were in and killed them all. My God, I cannot imagine. What blows my mind is what Job did. It states in *Job 1:20*, *"The scripture says Job arose, and rent his mantel, and shaved his head, and fell upon the ground, and worshipped."*

Job was a man that knew his God. As we look on down in *Job 1:22 it states*, *"In all this Job sinned not, nor charged God foolishly." Job 2:9 states, "Then said his wife unto him, Dost thou still retain thine integrity? curse God, and die."* From the beginning, Job pledged his allegiance to God and was rooted in knowing regardless of what happens God is more than enough. Job also had to contend with his three friends that more or less gave their human understanding of why he was suffering. His friends were inaccurate because they did not know God like Job. Sometimes friends mean well, and sometimes they can be a blessing or a lesson. We have to know God for ourselves because there will come a time, like Job, that we will stand alone.

In conclusion, God is separating and dividing. He is awakening our hearts to the days and times we are living. Will God be enough? Yes, our God is more than enough!

Journal 37 – Lest We Forget

Can you imagine bringing home the most beautiful baby boy, perfect, with beautiful big eyes that glow? Eyes that hold so much love that you become lost in the gaze of his beauty, a pure innocence that only comes from heaven? Would you be willing to lose or allow any harm to come to him?

I can't imagine how Father God felt gazing into the eyes of His only begotten Son, Jesus, knowingly and willingly having to offer Him up for you and me. This perfect little baby who was born in a manger had to be rejected by His Father because of the sin of man. Can you or I ever imagine seeing our son ripped from us, beat, rejected, crucified, denied, and hung to a cross for something he never did? Have you or I ever considered the cost of the cross and what it did to our heavenly Father? The scripture says even the disciples could not tarry one hour in prayer as Christ was in the trial of His life, praying not to go through the suffering He would have to endure because of our sin. When we truly come into reality of the cost of the cross because of sin, I'm certain it would have a profound effect on our lives, and we would not live so casually. Casual living meaning the love of self, living a life not ruled by the government of God, refusing to follow where the Spirit leads, rebellion to the Word, and half-heartedness.

I often hear others say that they will never forget the day my granddad died or my grandma died, but I never hear them say I will never forget the day Jesus died for me on Calvary. Nor do I

Lest We Forget

hear them say I will never forget all the suffering He went through for me, the price He paid, the day my whole life changed, how my burdens were lifted, and I have never been the same. I never hear it and to me something is wrong with that picture. I can't imagine what it took for God to send down that perfect little boy, the little wonder that changed the world and still today is a wonder.

Jesus became me on the cross, the unworthy sinner that had severely screwed my life up so bad and at one time, had made a thousand promises that I never kept. But one cold January day I was encountered by Christ, and my life has never been the same.

Hopefully, the world will never forget one event, and that is 9/11. Each year a memorial is held to honor the fallen and to remind us to never forget the grievous atrocity that was committed to the American people on our own soil. In retrospect, from this day forward may we remember by making a mental footnote imprinted upon our hearts the sacrifice, the innocent blood that Christ shed, and the price that Christ paid for us. May we never forget the nails hammered through His hands, the beatings, the public shame, the pain, and most importantly the love He had for us when He laid down His life for us? May we do as the Word says in ***Colossians 1:10, "That ye might walk worthy of the Lord unto all pleasing, being fruitful in every good work, and increasing in the knowledge of God."*** May we be aware that willful sinning is as a nail crucifying our Savior all over again, and His blood is being counted as no effect on our lives.

Awaken Oh Bride

The little baby boy that once laid in a manger is now seated at the right hand of His Father with all power, authority, and glory. He is now the Roaring Lion of the tribe of Judah and is soon returning. Jesus, oh what a wonder you are!

Journal 38 – Don't Be Wasteful

This journal is directed toward those who may be lagging behind in the race, and lost their fire and passion for God, because they went their own way without receiving God's blessings. Your thoughts may be what's the use. I understand exactly what you are going through in the reality of the situation. I have good news. Be encouraged. You are not alone. Don't worry, you're in good company. The prodigal son **(See Luke 15:11-32)** is a good example of what can happen when we go our own way without God's blessings. When the prodigal son had squandered all his wealth in wild living, and the choices he had made, it caused him to end up making a choice to either eat the pig's food or go back home and become a hired servant. With his back up against the wall of reality, he realized the pigs were eating better than he was, and so were the hired servants that worked for his father. The Word says the prodigal son finally **came to himself** and said he would be better off returning home to his father as a hired servant.

When the rubber meets the road no one but you or I can decide when we become fed up, come to ourselves, and do something about the situations in our lives. I am grateful the Lord renews His mercies every morning and His mercies outweigh all of our faults and failures. The story of the prodigal son clearly teaches us that regardless of how far you have drifted away there is hope. The wonderful news is God does not see us as man sees us. Hallelujah!

Perhaps I'm talking to some prodigals who are contemplating on returning to Christ and feel so down and ashamed because they don't believe God will accept them back. Lift up your heads and lay your life down. A laid down life is not one where we call the shots and decide from day to day what we choose to do when we want to do it.

It is that simple. Return with your whole heart and do not worry about what others say. Allow God to prove you. Come on and get in the race. For He that began a good work in you will perform it.

Journal 39 – Choices

One day while going through my closet trying to find something to wear to work the next day I paused, looked around trying to decide, and thought to myself, *I do have a lot of clothes to choose from.* As I continued trying to make some choices of what to wear, and not finding anything, I wanted to go and buy something else. I then asked the Lord what makes me sometimes want to buy when I have enough clothes and shoes already to choose from. I heard that each piece of clothing along with shoes, purses, and earrings is what makes an outfit. Each piece of clothing was a building block and it gave me a variety to choose from.

Each choice that you and I make builds things. It's no different spiritually because every choice that we make we are building something that will reach a specific end. The power to choose is a great privilege that must not be treated lightly. The Lord, in His graciousness, gave each of us free will which gives us the power to choose. He is a just God and will not violate our free will though sometimes He knows the things we choose are not always good and wise. Nonetheless, we have the power to choose.

The Lord in His goodness left us instructions (His Word) to follow in how we choose and its repercussions. In the book of **Deuteronomy 30:15 it reads**, **"Today I am giving you a choice between good and evil, between life and death."** Clearly, we see from this portion of scripture that depending on how we choose will depict what type of outcome we will have. Some choices we

Choices

make today could very well have an effect or impact on our lives immediately or in our future. I have heard the statement 'we make our choices and our choices make us.' It could not have been better said. The building blocks of choices face us each and every moment from the least to the greatest, such as do I want to buy a car, a house, accept this proposal (marry him or her), or serve the Lord.

Though times have continued to change rapidly, I now realize that some choices and decisions that I made will not suffice for the times in which I am currently living. When I first started walking with the Lord many years ago, I was not wholehearted toward God and some things that I once said such as "It don't take all that to serve God." I have now found out that yes it does! God wants our whole heart. While there is yet time God is asking the church to make a choice to live for Him completely and wholeheartedly because He wants to be first, and He is coming back for His Bride.

In the book of **_Joshua 24:15 it reads, "And if it seem evil unto you to serve the Lord, choose you this day whom ye will serve."_** Maybe today you and I once started out serving the Lord, but we never moved from a mere outer-court relationship where we were just church goers and not relational with God. When I was a kid, I remember a song we used to sing called Sunday's Child. The moral of the song was Sunday was the only day the child was a saint. On Monday, Tuesday, Wednesday, Thursday, Friday, and Saturday a Saint he AIN'T. That song speaks volumes of much of

Awaken Oh Bride

what I have encountered. ***1 Corinthians 10:21-23 says, "Ye cannot drink the cup of the Lord, and the cup of devils: ye cannot be partakers of the Lord's table, and of the table of devils. Do we provoke the Lord to jealousy? are we stronger than he? All things are lawful for me, but all things are not expedient: all things are lawful for me, but all things edify not."***

Once again, we can see the power of choices and the importance of our decisions. The Word is clear that we cannot drink of both cups, the cup of the Lord's and demons. At one time I thought that I could as I was a Sunday child. I served the Lord but my heart was far from Him and I was deceived the whole time. I am grateful for the Lord's mercy and kindness on my life while I was yet in darkness though I was a church goer and Bible toting believer. I am now certain if I had died, I would not have ended up in a good place.

Today the Lord is sounding the trumpet, can you hear it? The Lord is not looking for mental assent. He is looking for a heart change and commitment. Choose ye this day whom you will serve. The Lord stands willing and waiting to receive you. *Selah!*

Journal 40 – Is the Wait Worth the Weight?

Once upon a time I felt as though I was between a rock and a hard place as I struggled to make a decision. I struggled because I knew that though the decision was my choice, I wanted to be assured it was in the will of God. It made me wonder if the wait is worth the weight. Trust me, I have made many decisions that I thought were good decisions and in the will of God but later found out I was mistaken. Learning to walk in faith during my struggle was very challenging, but it made me stretch my faith and belief far beyond what I could see, taste, feel, or touch.

Yet, I am reminded of something the Apostle Paul said in *1 Corinthians 6:12: "All things are lawful unto me, but all things are not expedient: all things are lawful for me, but I will not be brought under the power of any."* Paul understood, though he had free will, he also knew the ramifications that some of his choices could lead to bondage and unnecessary weights.

Weights are considered to be burdens, earthly cares, pressures of life, and sin. *Hebrews 12:1: "Wherefore seeing we also are compassed about with so great a cloud of witnesses, let us lay aside every weight, and the sin which doth so easily beset us, and let us run with patience the race that is set before us."* Brothers and sisters, how we live matters and our choices and decisions really do matter. Weights impact our life in the spirit and

hinder us from being able to stay above any situation, circumstance, or trial.

At times I have experienced being drawn into a circumstance that was not of my own choosing, and it took everything for me not to allow the weight of the situation to weigh me down in the spirit. However, with the help of the Lord I was able to stay afloat in the spirit. While I was waiting on God to change the situation, He was changing me in the situation so the growth and increase of His son would be made manifest in me. The pressure in the midst of the trial is a process that produces warriors who will fight not to be pulled down by the weight of their trials.

I am forever reminded of *__2 Corinthians 21:17: "For our light affliction, which is but for a moment, worketh for us a far more exceeding and eternal weight of glory."__* Oh, how I desire the full weight of the Lord's glory, a fullness of His person shining brightly through me in power. It's all about Christ being revealed in and through us, the people of God. So today, we must ask ourselves, is the WAIT worth the WEIGHT of His glory?

May the Lord bless and keep you in the midst of unseemly circumstances and trials as you are being changed from glory-to-glory.

Journal 41 – A Living Sacrifice of Worship

> *"I beseech you therefore, brethren, by the mercies of God, that ye present your bodies a living sacrifice, holy, acceptable unto God, which is your reasonable service."* **(Romans 12:1)**

When you hear the word worship what comes to mind? Is it good music, something you do, the way you live, or the way you dress? Our lives must be a living sacrifice that's worth offering to the Father. To me, worship has almost become as a prop to reach God, and has fallen under the guise of good sounding music, flashing lights, panting, and dancing with worship leaders. Sadly, nothing could be further from the truth when the passage above clearly states worship is the offering of our bodies, holy and a living sacrifice.

Additionally, worship is about spiritual devotion to God, being set apart from the world and self. Worship means being holy in all manner of living and in all aspects of our lives. Worship is about a personal relationship with God. When we gather in our churches, the Word says with the fruit of our lips we are offering sacrifices of praise to God. **(See Hebrews 13:15)**

Every day, each moment, and every second is an opportunity for worship because it's minute by minute and moment by moment that we should submit our lives and yield to the Father. Then, we too can say as Christ, "Not my will but your will be done." That is

A Living Sacrifice of Worship

true worship. This shows our love for Him is proved by our worship and sacrifice.

However, some worship movements can draw people away from communion in the Spirit, which could lead to an appeasing of the flesh. After such a movement I have heard people say, boy the worship was great. It gave me goose bumps. Regrettably, I am not hearing them say the presence of the Lord was so strong and I was convicted in my spirit that I need to change some things in my life. However, the attention is not on God and it is a trick from the enemy. For some reason this type of church wants something for nothing, but true worship deals with the heart and the giving of ourselves.

People of God, I encourage you today to present your bodies as a living sacrifice, and be changed in the presence of a holy God.

Journal 42 – We Don't Back Down, We Pray Up

The storms of life are raging all around and within us. The majority of my life I feel as though I have always been in the eye of a storm that seeks to destroy me. However, I find that Christ has been with me in and through every storm and in the end, most have worked out to my advantage. Storms are a part of our maturing process because they put us through tests to determine if we truly love God. These tests remind me of the training of the armed forces. They are put to such extreme tests to be ready for any and every rescue operation. That's kind of the way a storm is in our lives. Its purpose is to prepare us for conflict and battle ahead as well as for our maturing in Christ.

I am reminded of Paul in Acts 27 when they had set sail by the coast of Asia. The sailing had become dangerous and Paul told the crew I perceive that this voyage will be with hurt and much damage, not only of the lading and ship, but also of our lives. As the tempestuous storm raged the angel of the Lord appeared to Paul and told him there would be no loss of life. Though the storm raged, they had to stay on the boat and ride through the storm in order to safely make it to land.

I too was going through a storm which pushed beyond my own limit. I became tired of fighting my own battles, and one day heard when trouble comes you don't back down you PRAY UP.

We Don't Back Down, We Pray Up

PRAY UP meaning you fight your battle on your knees looking to Christ for strength allowing Christ to increase in you to conquer the storm. The enemy would love nothing more than for us to throw up our hands, sit down, and cry, but NO! **WE DON'T BACK DOWN, WE PRAY UP!**

Perhaps you are in the midst of a storm of sickness, depression, homelessness, joblessness, friendless, or whatever, I encourage you to ride through these storms looking unto Jesus and allowing Him to conquer whatever storms you may be going through. I exalt you today my friends don't back down, but **PRAY UP,** knowing this too will work out for your good.

Journal 43 – Awaken and Arise

When you heard your alarm clock this morning how did you respond? Were you sluggish, did you let it sound awhile before hitting the snooze or stop button? Perhaps you have set one or more alarms in sequence to give you time to finally respond to the alarm or to the alert that it's time to awaken and get up. It's obvious that we live in a day of alarms and alert systems which have proven to be valuable and has saved lives. We have car alarms, phone alarms, fire alarms, missing person alert systems, home alarms, and many more.

However, my point is, alarms and alerts must be heeded if we expect to have good outcomes for ourselves, our families, and in our communities. We can see all through the scripture the Lord gave alerts and warnings of certain things to come. Being able to hear and see them both physically and spiritually is of utmost importance in the days we are now living. Most communities and companies today may have drills which are mandated in the event some unexpected circumstances occur. I have noticed that some people have become so immune to the drills and pay no attention to them because nothing ever seems to happen.

In the Word of God, we can see that when the Lord gave warnings the event did not always happen immediately which gave time for people to do the necessary preparations that would be required to be safe. We can read of such an instance in the book of Genesis about Noah. In Genesis, Chapter 6, Noah was commanded

Awaken and Arise

by God to build an ark because He was going to destroy all the earth by flood. Some say it took Noah one-hundred and twenty years to build the ark and people were told it was going to rain. The Lord, through Noah, was giving out an alarm, a warning call for people to prepare. Unfortunately, only Noah, his family, and two of each animal entered the ark. What a sad and devastating story for those that did not heed the alarm and warning. So, it is today in the year 2019 the Lord is sending out His alarm for people to awaken, if need be, return back to Him, and set their lives in order to prepare to meet Him in these last days.

Regardless if any of us are believers or not, whether we believe in the rapture, (the catching away of the church), we can all agree, that we can look out and see the world in which we are living in today that something is wrong. If we are honest with ourselves, we can agree with **Genesis 6:5: *"And God saw the wickedness of man was great in the earth and the every imagination of the thoughts of his heart was only evil continually."*** Don't know about your world, but that's the world I am living in and am looking forward to the coming of the Lord.

In my world is what **2 Timothy 2:4 says, *"Men are lovers of pleasure more than lovers of God."*** You may find thousands having pleasure glorifying their sports team, but unfortunately, rarely will you find thousands publicly praying and giving glory to God. However, something is wrong if there is no prayer when everything is going well in their city or in the lives of the people.

The warning in ***Joel 2:1: "Blow ye the trumpet in Zion, and sound an alarm in my holy mountain: let all the inhabitants of the land tremble: for the day of the LORD cometh, for it is nigh at hand."*** Regardless to popular opinion we are living in the last days and the day of preparation to meet the King is now. We don't wait for His arrival to start preparing; that's the whole purpose of an alarm! The Lord is sounding the alarm and it's time we awaken and repent of loving our lives and our world more than God. I believe it does us good to stop for a moment and take inventory of our lives and see what we hold dear and cling to and if that is or could be the possible thing that can save us or bring salvation. If not, it's time to let go and grab hold to God, the hour is late.

The reason for penning this book of journals is a mandate from heaven. The Lord says He wants His people to awaken, arise, and prepare as time is short. When a trumpet is sounded it is a loud noise meant to awaken His people. The Lord also told me that these journals were not to be traditional as to fit in the box of what man deems to be acceptable as He knew it would offend some but awaken many. God is a God of love and wishes that no man perishes, but that all would come to repentance. God is not a control freak that will force you into a decision as He gave each one of us free will to choose Him or the world.

However, I would like to encourage you to seek God for yourself and know that you are only responsible for you. Sadly, the

Awaken and Arise

majority will not follow because the Lord already told us in His Word the way is narrow and few there are that find it. More than likely you will have to go it alone. That has been my life's story. Most of what we hear preached is cotton candy and requires no conflict or the denying of oneself, but that couldn't be further from the truth. The crucifixion of our Lord shows us how to die and how to live. The cross is the only way, not some of the feel good inspirational sermons that cost us nothing.

Today we each stand at a crossroad. Will we hear the sound of the alarm and respond? Or will we hit the snooze button and sleep on into eternity having not prepared. Let us choose prayerfully and wisely. As my grandmother used to say, "It's time to straighten up and fly right." The Word tells us that it will be a great falling away, even though there is much talk about a great move of God. There will be a great falling away; it will become much darker in our world for the light to arise. Will you and I let God arise in us as light that God's enemies be scattered? You and I choose. **(See Psalm 68:1-3)**. *Selah!*

Journal 44 – Change

As I come to the close of this book of journals, my hope is that somewhere along the way you were encountered by Christ. I pray that some of the tools in this toolbox became useful for you. In closing, I am reminded of the parable of the sower **(see Matthew, Chapter 13)**. Some seeds fell by the wayside, some fell in stony places, some fell among thorns, and some fell on good ground. Anytime the seed of God's Word falls on good ground of the heart it will spring up some hundredfold, some sixtyfold, some thirtyfold. When the increase comes, change comes, and we are no longer the same. Change simply means to make different. We become different when the Word of God is allowed to grow and increase inside us.

As I said from the beginning, it was the Lord's direction to pen topics that were not heard much or were unpopular. Truth can be hard sometimes to hear or accept, but the fact is that truth is truth. The Lord is awakening His church and alerting her to the times we are now living in, the last days. The way we live must change once encountered with the truth if we are going to go with Him. It was not the Lord's intentions for me to pen these journals with the purposes of them only becoming just reading information, but for light and truth that prayerfully will lead to a transformation of change.

While sitting in the Lord's presence upon the closing of this last journal, the Lord spoke and said, "Change will be the enemy of the people in the end times." Change is hard and usually goes against our belief systems, the way we do and see things. Nonetheless, we must be willing to trust God and go all the way. Change is happening all around us every day in our lives and communities, and we will not be able to maneuver in these end times without being a people of change in the directions in which the Lord may lead any of us. It's a set apart time for a set apart people to and for God, and it will require great change. For instance, change was hard for the children of Israel when they left Pharaoh's house and headed for the Promised Land. They had trouble with the change in food, and the leader because they were unwilling to change and follow God. However, this is the day we are living in, the day of change, the day to draw nigh to God with all that is in us regardless of the cost. If you are waiting around for people to decide to go with you, it may be too late. If you are waiting to see how things are going to go, it may be too late. Our walk with the Lord is individual, and we cannot put our trust in the arms of the flesh.

The trumpet is sounding, and Christ is awakening His people to awakening a-way-out. Change is upon us my friends and I pray that Christ meets you somewhere off the pages of these journals. Christ said, **I Am the Way**, so we don't have to look for a way. He is all we will and ever need. Be blessed, and I pray your life will never be the same. **AWAKEN OH BRIDE!**

✍ A Message From the Author

This collection of journals will be a call for the church to awaken and arise. Arise to the new day dawning of *Isaiah 60:1*: **"Arise, shine; for thy light is come, and the glory of the Lord is risen upon thee."** The church has been in the shadows far too long—the shadows caused by sin and selfishness, which has dimmed our brightness.

Though the journey has been long, it's time for the church to remove the veils that cover her eyes and focus on Christ. The Lord has plans for His Bride and wants to make her ready, but there is a process of returning and refining that will be needed to make us a church without spot, or wrinkle, or any such thing.

If you are ready for the dawning of a new day; if you are prepared to prepare to meet the King, this book of journals is for you. Preparation is practical and a daily journey. We have entered into the end times. Thank you for coming with me on this journey as it's going to change your life for eternity. May *Awaken Oh Bride* rekindle your love for God, your passion, and cause the warrior within to arise and fight as we race toward the finish line of Jesus Christ. *Selah!*

✝ *Rochelle Butler*

www.ingramcontent.com/pod-product-compliance
Lightning Source LLC
Chambersburg PA
CBHW070949080526
44587CB00015B/2241